Daniel J. O'Hern

What Makes a Court Supreme

THE WILENTZ COURT
FROM WITHIN

DANIEL J. O'HERN

Contents

About the Author

Daniel J. O'Hern spent the bulk of his career in public service, holding positions that included town council member, mayor, gubernatorial cabinet official and chief counsel, and New Jersey Supreme Court justice. On the bench, he and his colleagues resolved some of the most complicated cases of the day, such as those involving equal educational opportunity, the right to die, exclusionary zoning and surrogate pregnancy.

Born in Red Bank, N.J., on May 23, 1930, O'Hern graduated from Fordham College in 1951 and then served in the Navy for three years, achieving the rank of lieutenant junior grade. His tour included duty aboard the *USS Essex* during the Korean War.

He graduated from Harvard Law School in 1957 and served as a law clerk to U.S. Supreme Court Justice William Brennan Jr. during the 1957-1958 term. O'Hern returned to Red Bank to practice with the firm of Vincent McCue and later with Abramoff, Apy and O'Hern. A Democrat, O'Hern was active in local politics, serving as a Red Bank councilman from 1962 until 1968 and as mayor from 1969 until 1978. Gov. Brendan T. Byrne named him commissioner of the Department of Environmental Protection in 1978 and his chief counsel in 1979. O'Hern became an associate justice on Aug. 6, 1981, replacing Mark A. Sullivan, who retired.

While on the Court, O'Hern served as chairman of the Judicial Salary and Pensions Committee, an adviser to the New Jersey Commission on Professionalism in the Law, chairman of the Family Court Reorganization Committee and a member of the Council of Judges of the National Council on Crime and Delinquency.

After he left the Court on May 23, 2000, at the mandatory retirement age of 70, O'Hern continued his service to the state and the legal profession. Beginning that year, he became a member of the New Jersey Advisory Committee on Judicial Conduct and the *New Jersey Law Journal*'s Editorial Board.

In 2004, he and Professor Paula A. Franzese of Seton Hall University School of Law were appointed special ethics counsel to Gov. Richard J. Codey. They submitted a comprehensive ethics audit and agenda, resulting in significant reform in the executive branch and promulgation of New Jersey's first Uniform Ethics Code.

At the time of his death on April 1, 2009, O'Hern was of counsel to the firm of Becker Meisel, working with his son Daniel J. O'Hern Jr. in the firm's Red Bank office. This book was completed shortly before he died.

Editor's Note

Daniel J. O'Hern served as an associate justice of the New Jersey Supreme Court from Aug. 6, 1981, until May 23, 2000. During that time, he saved memos from his colleagues, letters from Chief Justice Robert N. Wilentz to members of the Court, charts that outlined the pros and cons of cases during Court conferences, sketches by members about their day-to-day life together and oral arguments, and photographs of the justices, among other mementos. O'Hern used these keepsakes, his recollections, and notes to himself to form the foundation for this book, which looks at his years on the Wilentz Court and at the members who served with him.

O'Hern wrote this book to convey the traits that shape a quality court. He wanted future governors to know what made a cohesive, effective and admired bench, and to keep those qualities in mind when filling vacancies on New Jersey's highest tribunal.

Wilentz's attributes were at the top of O'Hern's list of necessary traits. The chief justice had the intellectual heft and the leadership ability to tackle some of the nation's most complex legal issues. O'Hern also tied the Wilentz bench's success to the collegial Court the chief justice created; Wilentz's graciousness, charm and wit led to an atmosphere that allowed the other members to flourish. They were a close group. It was not unusual for Wilentz to end personal notes to the others with "Love, Robert," or to send flowers or wine to their hotel rooms when they were on vacation. He also permitted the Court's closed-door debates to last for days so each member could feel that his or her viewpoint had been heard.

And that spirit of collegiality, in turn, shaped their decisions.

In the end, the traits O'Hern felt characterized a quality bench were the building blocks he found essential to his overall goal: public confidence in the judiciary and the legal profession. In his eyes, that was the way the Court achieved legitimacy.

— Pamela E. Brownstein
Executive Editor New Jersey Law Journal"

Acknowledgments

"A Poem for Seven Justices" was the title of an op-ed column by A.M. Rosenthal in *The New York Times* on Feb. 5, 1988. It was a piece about the New Jersey Supreme Court's opinion in the Baby M case over a surrogate mother's contract. Rosenthal wrote: "I wish I could write or commission a poem for Chief Justice Robert N. Wilentz and his six colleagues on the Supreme Court of the State of New Jersey. They gave us all some happy news by voting 7 to 0 that mercy, compassion and human dignity are indeed part of the law and must be observed — particularly by judges."

Of course, to us the case was not about mercy and compassion, but about the limits of the law and the ability of a person to sell a child. Still, Rosenthal's column was a moving tribute. I always thought of writing that poem. This is it, without rhyme.

I acknowledge and thank the law reviews of Rutgers University School of Law in Newark and Camden and Seton Hall University School of Law, in whose pages many of the portraits of the justices first appeared.

I also acknowledge the help of two of my law clerks, Holly English and Dena Reger, who assisted and encouraged me in writing these recollections. Special thanks go to Will Reger, who did some of the early graphics for the book. I thank Justice Robert L. Clifford, who proofread these pages as he proofread my opinions.

Finally, I thank *New Jersey Law Journal* Publisher Robert Steinbaum and Executive Editor Pamela Brownstein. They encouraged me to publish these recollections in the *Law Journal*. Pamela is the one who put it together.

My purpose is not to excite the public about the human frailties of the justices. Everything in the book is within the public domain or of such a nature that my colleagues would not regard its disclosure as a breach of the trust that is necessary to the functioning of a collegial court. We trusted each other implicitly.

My goal is to illustrate the qualities that make a person a great judge on an ensemble court. My hope is to encourage future governors and senators to seek the appointment of extraordinary people who will preserve the excellence of the New Jersey Supreme Court.

1

Introduction

M ost readers of this tribute are probably familiar with the decisions of the Wilentz Court in areas such as equal educational opportunity, the right to die, exclusionary zoning and lawyer discipline. I will speak of them, but not exhaustively. Primarily, I want to emphasize how those decisions were shaped by the type of Court run by Chief Justice Robert N. Wilentz, particularly his warm and close relationship with the associate justices.

Although we had feared for his health, the news we received on June 24, 1996, still came as a shock to us. I was in the library of my office in Red Bank when my secretary, Carol Rittershofer, called to say that the Chief Justice was on the telephone. It was a beautiful summer morning and I could see the Navesink River sparkle in the sunlight outside my window. The contrast between our settings was painful. The Chief Justice was speaking from his room at Mount Sinai Medical Center in New York City. He had been there since late May with a troubling condition that had first manifested itself as a foot disorder.

The members of the Court had last seen the Chief Justice on May 23 at his home in Deal, where we held part of that day's conference as a convenience to him. As we walked onto the porch, he greeted each of us with warmth, but his pain was immediately apparent. He moved from the porch to the dining room with a noticeable limp, though nevertheless led our discussion with humor and precision. It was the last conference we were to attend with him.

When the Chief Justice called me on June 24, he said he would submit his resignation to Gov. Christine Todd Whitman later that morning. He had called each member of the Court in order of seniority, telling us that cancer had spread throughout his body and that he no longer could carry out his duties. He wished us each to know before the official announcement was made. I was struck by his unfailing courtesy in calling each of us personally. When I said it was so unfair he should fall sick just eight months before retirement, the 69-year-old Chief Justice replied, "I am an old man, Dan." More than anything, that remark conveyed to me a sense of his suffering. Until then, except when especially burdened, he had presided over the Court with a boyish charm. The charm was gone. Cancer of the brain had robbed him of his health. I called Carol into the library and told her what the Chief Justice had told me. We had feared as much when he had written me about a week before concerning one of the last opinions of the term, in which his was the crucial fourth vote. He had enclosed his usual insightful comments on the circulating opinion, made several substantive additions and concluded, "Dan, you'd better file this quickly."

Almost every member who sat on the Court with Robert Wilentz has described his or her reaction to his resignation. Each of us was overcome with grief. We had lost a leader, a colleague and a friend. Later in the day, my son Jim called to ask how I was. I said it was terrible to think that the Chief lay dying and that our 15-year service together was over. Jim said, "You had a great run."

It was a great run and this book is the story of that run, and primarily of the years from the beginning of 1985 through the end of 1994, a period in which the Court's composition was unchanged. The Wilentz Court was often described as the nation's best state tribunal. Professor Laurence Tribe of Harvard Law School said it was the best appellate court in the country, state or federal. What made the Court "supreme"? Simply the men and women whom a series of great governors — with the advice and consent of the Senate — entrusted with the preservation of the traditions of independence, integrity and excellence that have characterized the New Jersey Supreme Court since the adoption of the 1947 Constitution.

I scribbled down these notes through the years, not to embarrass anyone, but to explain how gifted these men and women were.

2

The Chief

For each one of us, there was an overwhelming moment of sadness when Chief Justice Wilentz informed us he would have to retire. Over time, our grief was tempered by the realization that we had been privileged to share in an extraordinary life. At the time of his death on July 23, 1996, I wrote in a tribute that was published in several newspapers:

There was no one like Chief Justice Wilentz — no one could write so powerfully; no one could question so skillfully; no one could lead so forcefully.

He had the natural gift of a great mind. He had natural and acquired qualities of leadership. He had the acquired virtue of absolute and uncompromising honesty. He had the unfailing courtesy never to belittle any of our arguments (and I was the worst offender when it came to making preposterous arguments).

He had immense personal charm. Unless burdened by one of those long nights of work and worry, he enlivened our Conferences with a wry sense of humor that pierced any pretense in our discussions.

To be with him was a pleasure. We knew of the lives of each of his children and each of their spouses, and even the names of some of the grandchildren — Gabriel and Raphael. We told him that he was running out of archangels. We knew about his mother-in-law and what she really thought about his opinions.

We even knew about his tomato crop. He consulted with us on each blight that threatened it.

A reporter asked me if he had any failings. I told him that I thought that the Chief Justice may have failed to appreciate how much he was loved by the people with whom he shared his life — his personal staff, his many clerks, the Administrative Director of the Courts, and, yes, the Justices.

PHOTO BY BILL KOSTROUN

The New Jersey Supreme Court's makeup remained unchanged from January 1985, when Gary Stein was appointed, until December 1994, when Robert Clifford retired. Left to right in this 1985 photograph are (top row) Marie Garibaldi, Stewart Pollock, Daniel O'Hern and Stein, and (bottom row) Clifford, Robert Wilentz and Alan Handler.

The family of Chief Justice Robert N. Wilentz has lost a wonderful father, grandfather and brother.

The New Jersey Supreme Court has lost a powerful leader whose last written words were of concern for the Court's independence.

Those of us who lived and worked with him have lost a warm and wonderful companion. It was enough to have known him.

Of all the things that made the New Jersey Court supreme, Chief Justice Wilentz was by far the most important. I have often thought of how best to describe his effect on the Court. The only helpful analogy is to an orchestra conductor. As Toscanini could bring out the best in each of the musicians, the Chief could bring out the best in each of us.

He was born to privilege on Feb. 17, 1927. His father, David T. Wilentz, was a successful lawyer in Middlesex County and, as chairman of the State Democratic Committee and a Democratic national committeeman, a leader in the Democratic Party. As New Jersey attorney general in 1935, he prosecuted Bruno Richard Hauptmann, the kidnapper of the Lindbergh baby. By all accounts, Robert spent a remarkably happy childhood in his native Perth Amboy, with summers spent in Deal.

According to Robert Fishkin, a boyhood friend, the Wilentz family was the first in Perth Amboy to own a television set. In a Nov. 8, 1995, interview with the Oral History Archives of World War II project, conducted by

Rutgers University, Fishkin recalled being invited to the Wilentzes' home in Deal:

> They had a house right on the ocean, right across from the Deal Beach Club. The house had two concrete lions in front ... in those days if any of the girls involved had been asked to go to someone's house for a weekend, the mothers would automatically say no. But since it was the Wilentzes' house, then everybody said "go."

Fishkin remembered attending a graduation party:

> We walked in and we see this table ... set for ten people and two servants and the big master plates underneath the service plates that you never use with the gold rims on them. And the whole works! [Afterwards], Mr. Wilentz gave Robert a $100 bill. "Go have a good time." So we went ... and I remember there was change left afterwards.

It was at Deal that Robert Wilentz met Jacqueline Malino, the girl next door, the love of his life. Jackie's parents had a summer house in Deal behind the Wilentzes' home. Fishkin recalled, "she was very well-educated ... [a] great woman."

For almost seven years, the members of the Court watched her gradually succumb to cancer. Often the Court's conferences were interrupted by telephone calls from Jackie, and we could not help overhearing the many anxious discussions about medical reports and upcoming appointments. During all this time, the Chief Justice displayed an enormous affection for his wife and accompanied her to radiation treatments. She died in 1989. I can think of no husband whose devotion exceeded that of the Chief.

He was a brilliant student. After graduation from Perth Amboy High School, he spent a year at Princeton University before serving for two years in the Navy. One of the many inside jokes on the Court involved my efforts to inject nautical metaphors into the Court's discussions, suggesting to the Court, for example, that it should "keep an anchor to windward" when troublesome situations arose. Those comments aroused a mock interest on the part of the Chief Justice. On one occasion, he described to us his attempt to climb the mast of a ship to repair the radar equipment, an effort that convinced him his career should be on dry land.

After he left the service, he went to Harvard College and graduated in 1949. He probably could have entered any law school in the country but chose Columbia because it kept him closer to Jackie. In his Vanderbilt Lecture to the Harvard Law School Association of New Jersey on Nov. 16, 1995, he said: "I assume I would have applied to the Law School, but for the fact that New York had certain attractions for me, especially the woman who was soon to be my wife. I am sure that, had I gone to Harvard, I would not have made half the mistakes that I did."

Upon graduation from law school in 1952, he joined his father's law firm, Wilentz, Goldman & Spitzer in Perth Amboy, which later moved to Woodbridge. He was not troubled by nepotism in law firms. He told us that as soon as he passed the bar, "Pop called me into his office and said, 'Robert, you're a partner now.'"

PHOTO BY THE STAR-LEDGER

When Gov. Brendan Byrne, right, nominated him to the Court in 1979, Robert Wilentz had been in private practice for 27 years, handling complex litigation and arguing major constitutional cases before the justices.

No amount of privilege spared him the burden of living up to his expectations of what a lawyer should be. As a practicing lawyer, he was known at the firm for all-nighters, during which he would enlist the support of teams of lawyers for the complex litigation he handled. For 27 years, he was a leading practitioner in the state. He argued important constitutional cases before the New Jersey Supreme Court, including *New Jersey State Chamber of Commerce v. New Jersey Election Law Enforcement Commission*, which held that the New Jersey Campaign Contributions and Expenditures Reporting Act's reporting and financial disclosure requirements for groups working to influence legislation do not violate the First Amendment. The Court also found that a $100 enforcement threshold was too low and an invalid exercise of administrative authority. The Chief Justice often teased Justice Alan B. Handler, the author of that opinion, about the "judicial surgery" performed by the Court to sustain the legislation. He also played a prominent role in New Jersey's public life and was elected to the New Jersey Assembly in 1965. His political career ended four years later when he announced his support for conflict-of-interest legislation. It required him to retire from the Assembly because it would have barred his firm's representation of public agencies.

Many legends surround the circumstances of Gov. Brendan T. Byrne's appointment of the Chief Justice in July 1979. (Gov. Byrne jokingly said at the time that he had done so on the basis of Robert's tennis ability. Robert had won several amateur tournaments, although Justice Robert L. Clifford liked to remind him that he was the only kid in Perth Amboy who owned a tennis racket.) It is certain to me that Robert Wilentz did not seek the office of Chief Justice. He said at the time that he had never thought of becoming a judge of any kind. I have no idea whether his father sought the office for him. At the time of the appointment, I said to his father, "You must be very proud that your son has become the Chief Justice of the New Jersey Supreme Court." He looked at me, smiled and, implying that the firm would miss his son's rain-making abilities in the years ahead, said, "He just talked me into signing a long lease on a new office building."

On a serious note, Gov. Byrne once told me that he had spoken with many lawyers who had said Robert Wilentz was simply "the best lawyer in New Jersey."

What were the qualities in Chief Justice Wilentz that helped make the Court supreme?

First, he had courage. From the beginning, he set his course on a distant star, universal respect for the judiciary and for lawyers. In *In re Commitment of Edward S.*, he explained why hearings on the continued commitment of the criminally insane had to be open to the public, despite the interests of confidentiality in mental health matters:

> Just as obviously, however, public confidence in the administration of criminal justice is of towering importance, and when it can be legitimately accommodated, it should be. ... All of these things are both indicators and causes of the public's concern about the legitimacy of the criminal justice system and its operation; all of them go to the question of the vulnerability of public confidence in our system of criminal justice. All of them go to the heart of this most important interest, namely, maintaining public confidence. One of the most important obligations of government, and in particular of the judiciary, is to legitimately preserve public confidence.

In *In re Wilson*, his first opinion, he explained why disbarment would almost invariably result when an attorney knowingly misappropriated client funds:

11

It is therefore important that we reemphasize that the principal reason for discipline is to preserve the confidence of the public in the integrity and trustworthiness of lawyers in general. This reason for discipline is mentioned in some misappropriation cases and not in others. While it may only rarely have been stressed in the past, we are now inclined to view it as controlling in these cases.

We have no doubt that the bar is as anxious as we are to preserve that trust. Its preservation is essential to public acceptance of reforms that may be proposed by the bench and bar together. Mistrust may provoke destructive change. Public confidence is the only foundation that will support constructive reform in the public interest while preserving the finest traditions of the profession. From that point of view, anything less than strict discipline in cases like this would be a disservice to the bar, the judiciary and the public.

Public confidence in the integrity of lawyers and judges was the foundation for everything the Court did. Essential to that public confidence was the complete independence of the judiciary. On Jan. 29, 1990, the Supreme Court publicly reprimanded two Superior Court judges for attending the Inaugural Ball honoring Gov. James J. Florio. In the accompanying statement, the Chief Justice observed:

There is no principle governing the judiciary in this state more firmly established or more important than the total separation of judges from politics. See *Clark v. DeFino*, 80 *N.J.* 539, 547, 404 *A.2d* 621 (1979); *In re Gaulkin*, 69 *N.J.* 185, 191 (1976); *In re Hayden*, 41 *N.J.* 443 (1964); *In re Pagliughi*, 39 *N.J.* 517 (1963). The principle is an essential ingredient of judicial independence; it is probably the most important requirement for maintaining public confidence in the judiciary. The rule is so clear, the tradition in this state so strong, that it is rarely violated. In New Jersey, judges and politics do not mix — not at all, either in fact or appearance.

The independence that inspires public confidence requires courage. To sail with a following wind is easy; to sail into the winds of political criticism is not as easy. Chief Justice Wilentz's clear vision of the role of the judiciary gave him the courage to lead an independent judiciary. He did not regard courts as spectators at public events, detached from the constitutional guarantees they must enforce. He would not allow the judiciary to become a tool to suppress society's less fortunate. The Chief Justice had the courage to enforce the Constitution when its guarantees were ignored. He said quite simply, in *Southern Burlington County N.A.A.C.P. v. Mount Laurel Township*:

> [T]here being a constitutional obligation, we are not willing to allow it to be disregarded and rendered meaningless by declaring that we are powerless to apply any remedies other than those conventionally used.

Next in importance among the qualities that elevated the Court was leadership, administrative and intellectual. As an administrator, Chief Justice Wilentz displayed boundless energy. He revitalized the New Jersey judiciary. After a national search, he recruited Robert D. Lipscher, the circuit executive of the Second U.S. Circuit Court of Appeals, to serve as administrative director of the courts. A rapid succession of administrative changes followed. The Chief Justice created a commission to investigate racial and ethnic bias in the courts, the New Jersey Supreme Court Task Force on Minority Concerns, which issued its status report in 1991. The next year, he adopted the recommendations by the Committee on Efficiency in the Operations of the Courts for improving the judiciary's delivery of services. He initiated the first American study of gender bias in the judiciary, the 1982 New Jersey Supreme Court Task Force on Women in the Courts. He also oversaw a reorganization of the attorney disciplinary system, overhauled civil and criminal case administration, and nurtured the development of a Family Part.

Above all, Chief Justice Wilentz was the intellectual leader of the Court, respected by its members. It may be possible to think of great courts that have not had great intellectual leaders, but I believe history points to the opposite premise. Consider the courts of New York, California and Massachusetts when led, respectively, by Chief Judge Benjamin N. Cardozo, Chief Judge Roger J. Traynor and Chief Justice Oliver Wendell Holmes Jr. During a period of great social change, Chief Justice Wilentz authored the signature opinions of the Court: *Mount Laurel*, which required developing towns to provide their fair share of affordable housing for the poor; *Abbott v. Burke*, which declared the state school-aid formula unconstitutional because it failed to provide sufficient funding for the poorest districts; *Kelly v. Gwinnell*, which held that a social host who provides alcohol to an intoxicated guest before he or she gets behind the wheel may be liable for injuries caused by the driver; and *New Jersey Coalition Against War in the Middle East v. J.M.B. Realty Corp.*, which held that the right of free speech in the state Constitution requires regional malls to permit, subject to reasonable conditions, leafleting and the exchange of ideas in these centers of commerce.

The Chief Justice was a rationalist, not an ideologue. At some point in my judicial career, I thought that Vaclav Havel embodied all the virtues of a public servant and I sent the Chief two of Havel's articles. The Chief, who was not a hero-worshiper nor given to abstraction, responded:

TO: JUSTICE DANIEL J. O'HERN

FROM: Chief Justice Robert N. Wilentz

RE: OP-ED HAVEL ARTICLE

DATE: August 3, 1992

I've read the March 1 op-ed Havel article. I am not prepared at this moment to go on to the next one, but I will later, but for the moment will content myself with some brief comments:

1. I had a low-grade fever for a few days. I suspect the article will cause a slight temperature rise.

2. Some of us must find the key, the meaning, the essence, the source, the truth, the polestar or we are not content. I am pleased that, for the moment, Havel is your truth. I only fear for the future. He cannot do much harm.

3. My respect for the Slovaks has increased greatly.

4. On that subject, Joe E. Lewis, a great philosopher who never sought too many truths, once said "show me a broke Slovak and I'll show you a bum check," or something like that.

5. Joe E. Lewis, incidentally, also remarked, when his doctor told him that he had better cut down on his drinking, that "all I know is that when I drive down the street I see a lot more old drunks than old doctors."

6. Beware — think hard — whenever deep thought is propped up by references to a Being.

7. Mr. Havel's main thesis appears to be that mankind is emerging from, or is at the end of, an era in which it mistakenly thought it had found the key to progress, inevitable progress, and that that key was rationality, science, planning, all the things you did when you were a Commissioner [of the Department of Environmental Protection]. Havel says there is

no such key, it is arrogant to assume there is one. That is, with one exception: Havel's key. He thinks if we'll only be a little bit more human, a little bit more personal, have a little bit more feeling, show a little bit more justice, respond to our own instincts, have a little sense of justice, in other words do all of the things I do in every one of my opinions, the world will be better off, not only that, but that's the key — especially if it is accompanied by some "humility in the face of the mysterious order of Being." He doesn't refer to those of us whose humility goes so deep that it exists forever without even being aware of the mysterious order.

8. I agree with Mr. Havel that we must try harder to understand than to explain, with one exception: I think Mr. Havel should try harder to explain.

9. More later.

R.N.W.

P.S. I have succumbed and read the other article. It adds very little. He is a very nice man, he may be deep, very profound, but my impression is that while not superficial, his observations, point of view, and "philosophy" are not really of any great depth. They are the reflections of an artist, and the real beauty and impact stem from the fact of his experience — the artist placed at the head of state so that everything that he says, the things that would provide interesting chitchat at the local tavern when exchanged with other artists, somehow take on great significance. I really don't think they have any such significance. That becomes clearer, at least to me, when this artist/statesman comes to the not-so-earthshaking revelation that there are some serious difficulties of a moral dimension to those who try to be moral in the political world. He had trouble signing legislation he didn't really approve of, and this was a great revelation to him. That kind of conflict is something even lowly Justices of a state court live with every day of the week, yet to him it is momentous and revealing.

Robert Wilentz reorganized the attorney discipline system and created panels to investigate racial, ethnic and gender bias in the courts.

I like him, he's nice, he's honest, but I hope by this Fall you have another hero. Before you pick one, may I just give you one warning: There's nothing wrong with computers, there's nothing wrong with people who serve in state or national or city government (bureaucrats), there's nothing wrong with trying to do the best you can and looking to the future (planning). Stupid mistakes can be made by using too few people and too little technology just as much as by using too many people and all possible technology. There's nothing whatsoever wrong with thinking as hard as you can, even if it's a little painful and hard work. The fact that one feels something very strongly doesn't mean it's right, as a matter of fact it's a good habit when you get that feeling to examine even more closely than usual what you're about to do. Especially if that feeling is one of dislike, contempt, and most of all, certainty.

I was always amazed by the ease with which Chief Justice Wilentz addressed constitutional problems. He wrote of constitutional doctrine in the manner of one describing a familiar landscape. He had an effortless recall of the core principles of constitutional law. His style was not encumbered by laborious citations that disrupt the flow of analysis. In *New Jersey Coalition Against War in the Middle East*, he used this engaging style to balance free-speech interests of antiwar protesters and property interests of suburban shopping mall owners:

There is no doubt about the outcome of this balance. On the one side, the weight of the private property owners' interest in controlling and limiting activities on their property has greatly diminished in view of the uses permitted and invited on that property. The private property owners in this case, the operators of regional and community malls, have intentionally transformed their property into a public square or market, a public gathering place, a downtown business district, a community; they have told this public in every way possible that the property is theirs, to come to, to visit, to do what they please, and hopefully to shop and spend; they have done so in many ways, but mostly through the practically unlimited permitted public uses found and encouraged on their property. The sliding scale cannot slide any farther in the direction of public use and diminished private property interests.

On the other side of the balance, the weight of plaintiff's free speech interest is the most substantial in our constitutional scheme. Those interests involve speech that is central to the purpose of our right of free speech. At these centers, free speech, such as leafleting, can be exercised without discernible interference with the owners' profits or the shoppers' and non-shoppers' enjoyment. The weight of the free speech interest is thus composed of a constant and a variable: the constant is the quality of free speech, here free speech that is the most important to society; the variable is its potential interference with this diminished private property interest of the owner. Given the limited free speech right sought, leafleting accompanied only by that speech normally associated with and necessary for leafleting, and subject to the owners' broad power to regulate, that interference, if any, will be negligible.

In a similarly unfettered manner, he explained in *Abbott v. Burke* II why the Thorough and Efficient Education Clause of the New Jersey Constitution required equal funding for the adequate education of the state's students:

Thorough and efficient means more than teaching the skills needed to compete in the labor market, as critically important as that may be. It means being able to fulfill one's role as a citizen, a role that encompasses far more than merely registering to vote. It means the ability to participate fully in society, in the life of one's community, the ability to appreciate music, art, and literature, and the ability to share all of that with friends. As plaintiffs point out in so many ways, and tellingly, if these courses are not integral to a thorough and efficient education, why do the richer districts invariably offer them? The disparity is dramatic. Alongside these basic-skills districts are school systems offering the broadest range of courses, instruction in numerous languages, sophisticated mathematics, arts, and sciences at a high level, fully equipped laboratories, hands-on computer experience, everything parents seriously concerned for their children's future would want, and everything a child needs. In these richer districts, most of which have some disadvantaged students, one will also find the kind of special attention and educational help so badly needed in poorer urban districts that offer only basic-skills training. If absolute equality were the constitutional mandate, and "basic skills" sufficient to achieve that mandate, there would be little short of a revolution in the suburban districts when parents learned that basic skills is what their children were entitled to, limited to, and no more.

It was not just the Chief Justice's opinions that made the Court great. He had the ability, born of years of trial practice, to unravel cases during oral argument. One of the distinguishing features of the New Jersey Supreme Court is endless oral argument.

Although we usually assigned each side 30 minutes, it was not at all unusual for argument to last for several hours.

An insightful example of the Chief's questioning occurred during the argument of *State v. Marshall* II, concerning a statutory amendment to limit the Court's proportionality review of death sentences to that class of cases in which the death sentence had been imposed. The Chief Justice graciously skewered the deputy attorney general's argument. He asked how, if the Court were to look only at death-sentenced cases, it could possibly know whether the death sentence for a particular case was aberrational. If the Court cannot know whether a particular death sentence is aberrational, the Court cannot know

PHOTO FROM NEW JERSEY LAW JOURNAL ARCHIVES

It was not unusual for Robert Wilentz to write 15-page, single-spaced memos about cases or administrative matters or to send faxes well past midnight, even near the end of his life. sentence had been imposed.

whether it is disproportionate. The Court concluded that the universe of cases to be considered in assessing the proportionality of death sentences must consist of all death-eligible cases.

Of all the Court's decisions during Chief Justice Wilentz's tenure, the ruling in *In the Matter of Baby M*, issued in 1988, gave me the greatest personal satisfaction. This case presented profound social issues concerning the contract of a surrogate mother to deliver to the biological father custody of the child she had borne. Lost in the conflict between the natural parents were the interests of the child. The Court's decision, authored by the Chief Justice, so ably set forth the controlling principles of law balancing the interests of mother, child and father that it achieved almost universal acclaim. In "A Poem for Seven Judges," a column in *The New York Times* on Feb. 5, 1988, commentator A.M. Rosenthal wrote:

> Most of the important news stories journalists deal with are sad or dreary. ...

> But once in a while something happens that sings of creativity or energy or wit or simple goodness and insists on taking hold of us and making us feel happy. ...

> I wish I could write or commission a poem for Chief Justice Robert N. Wilentz and his six colleagues on the Supreme Court of the State of New Jersey. They gave us all some happy news by voting 7 to 0 that mercy, compassion and human dignity are indeed part of the law and must be observed — particularly by judges.

> The decision was about paying a woman to bear a child; illegal, they ruled, in the State of New Jersey. It was also about the rights of motherhood. They ruled that no contract could be enforced that deprives a mother of her parental rights, not in New Jersey.

Another of the Chief Justice's gifts to the Court was the gift of understanding — understanding of the relationship of law to the community around us. During a speech on June 8, 1995, at the graduation ceremony of the William J. Brennan Jr. American Inn of Court, he told the young lawyers:

> Get to know as many people as you can possibly get to know — all kinds of people. Talk to them, eat with them, drink with them if you are so inclined. Just get to know as many people as there are. In that way you will understand more about people and more about life, more about things that people think about, and you will be a much more capable lawyer.

And, I would say, a more capable judge.

In his 1991 address to the graduates of the Rutgers University School of Law in Newark, the Chief reflected on the divisions in our society. He saw a collection of islands separated by race, ethnicity and poverty — a situation he yearned to end or at least improve. He told the students:

> The problem is deep, severe, crippling to a good society. And we are a good society. My concern is the possibility that we may accept this reality. My concern is that we may accept this condition as something we are willing to live with permanently. My concern is that when you see something, no matter how horrible, when you see it long enough and often enough, you stop seeing how horrible it is. The separateness of our society

is horrible, its disparate wealth and education is horrible, and it is not getting better. We must not become blind to it. We must see it and we must deal with it. Not in order to become rich, not in order to become safe, not even to be fair — although all of that — but to be a happy society, at home with each other, at ease with each other, friends and neighbors, not enemies; not at arm's length, but hand in hand. The causes are complex but at this point in history we don't need to fix blame. There is enough to go around for all of us. We need to fix society.

He also believed strongly in the right of society to protect itself. In 1983, he wrote *State v. DesMarets*, which affirmed mandatory criminal sentencing. In 1995, he wrote *Doe v. Poritz*, upholding Megan's Law, which requires community notification of the presence of sex offenders. As this excerpt from *Poritz* shows, he was not soft on crime:

[W]e remain convinced that the statute is constitutional. To rule otherwise is to find society is unable to protect itself from sexual predators … . That the remedy has a potentially severe effect arises from no fault of government, or of society, but rather from the nature of the remedy and the problem.

Another gift to the Court was the Chief's dignity. He knew what was required to keep the Court great in the public's mind. That commitment to dignity was illustrated in his handling of two of the Court's greatest unpublished opinions. The case, *State v. Valentine*, involved the reasonableness of a police search of a young man who had paused to relieve himself behind a tree. The state asserted that these were suspicious circumstances giving cause for a warrantless arrest. A majority of the Court agreed and was prepared to sustain the search.

PHOTO BY BILL KOSTROUN

Robert Wilentz advised young lawyers to get to know as many people as possible, and from a spectrum of backgrounds, as a way of becoming more capable in their practices.

Justice Clifford wrote a tongue-in-cheek dissent reflecting on the urinary tract problems of men and the reasons they might be impelled to seek the cover of a tree. He reasoned that there was nothing suspicious at all about hiding behind a tree to relieve oneself:

RE-CIRC. BY FAX 1-13-94 SUPREME COURT
OF NEW JERSEY
A-39 September Term 1993

STATE OF NEW JERSEY,
Plaintiff-Appellant,

v.

RONALD VALENTINE,
Defendant-Respondent.

Argued November 9, 1993 – Decided
On appeal from the Superior Court, Appellate Division

Deborah Bartolomey, Deputy Attorney General, argued the cause for appellant (Fred DeVesa, Acting Attorney General of New Jersey, attorney).

Neal M. Frank, Designated Counsel, argued the Cause for respondent (Zulima V. Farber, Public Defender, attorney).

CLIFFORD, J., dissenting.

The Court's opinion, with its intimation of incredulity, ante at_____,___(slip op. at 3, 20), at defendant's claim that he ducked behind a tree to relieve himself even though he was but a short distance from home, reads as if no member of the majority has ever experienced the sudden, urgent demand of nature's call and the pressing need for an immediate — I mean immediate — response. I have, so I am not about to join in the Court's unquestioning acceptance of Officer Nuccio's disbelief of defendant's explanation of his conduct. See also William Shakespeare, Macbeth act 2, sc. 3, 25-38 (Sylvan Barnet ed., Signet Classic 1986) (discussing effects of overindulgence); cf. The Unfriendly Skies, A.B.A. J., Jan. 1994, at 33 (quoting Associated Press's report of scolding by Chief Judge Norman C. Roettger, Jr., of the U.S. District Court for the Southern District of Florida, of prosecutors who had allowed a German tourist to remain in jail for nine months before his sentencing on a charge of interfering with flight crew: "The intoxicated tourist told a flight attendant 'the roof would go' if he wasn't permitted to use the bathroom, which she took to be a bomb threat. Roettger said the phrase was a German colloquialism that meant his bladder was about to explode.").

As for the outpouring of my concurring colleague, his argument simply does not hold water. Because his flow of words seems unimpeded by any mid-stream reflection of real-life experience, I can only express the hope that the serenity with which he accepts today's maculation of the law will see him through the little physical surprises that I for one am certain await him in his fast-approaching maturity.

Moreover, I am not impressed, as the majority apparently is, <u>ante</u> at_____,_(slip op. at 3, 20), by defendant's failure to have made eye contact with the officer. Defendant might not succeed as a jut-jawed stand-in for Arnold Schwarzenegger as the Terminator or Terminator 2, but fluttering eyes and milquetoast demeanor do not a villain make.

For me, the case comes down to a challenge to our ingenuity in teasing out of this slim record a range of nuances of conduct and speech that lead to a result favoring either admissibility or suppression. Had the issue come to us on a petition for certification rather than as an appeal of right under <u>Rule</u> 2:2-1(a), I very much doubt that we would have taken the case. The controlling principles of law are firmly established; the problem arises with their application in an acutely fact-sensitive area. Because I think the majority in the court below has the better of the argument on that score, I would affirm substantially for the reasons set forth in its opinion.

Justice Handler composed a droll reply that addressed with equal humor the vagaries of the human condition:

Circulated: 1/10/94
SUPREME COURT OF NEW JERSEY
A-39 September Term 1993

STATE OF NEW JERSEY
Plaintiff-Appellant,
v.
RONALD VALENTINE,
Defendant-Respondent.

HANDLER, J., concurring.

I concur in the opinion of the Court, which holds that under all the circumstances — defendant's unusual conduct and actions, his facile explanation, the lateness of the hour, defendant's criminal record, and the high-crime environment — Officer Nuccio had an adequate basis for an investigatory stop and pat-down search.

I would add the observation, fully noted by the Court, ante at_____ (slip op. at_____), that the necessity for the limited search in this case does not arise solely from the fact that defendant was found in a high-crime area. Other factors combined to make him a justified object of suspicion. E.g., State in the Interest of H.B., 75 N.J. 243, 268 (1977) (Handler, J., dissenting) ("A founded and solid feeling that a person is an armed criminal cannot be predicated simply upon the proposition that crime is rampant in densely populated states and congested cities. Rather, it must emanate from specific and articulable facts pointing a straight finger of suspicion at the individual.").

Further, with the Court I share Officer Nuccio's disbelief of defendant's explanation of his suspicious, furtive behavior. The dissent reminds us that the urgent demands of the bladder are visited without distinction on the righteous as well as the reprobate. The dissent may have reason to be more compassionate for those who suffer from the tyranny of the bladder. Nevertheless, common sense should not be supplanted by the micturations of a neurogenic bladder or the expertise of a lithotomist or urologist in assessing the veracity of defendant's allegations. When asked what he was doing by Officer Nuccio, defendant responded that he was "about to urinate, until he saw the police vehicle." Officer Nuccio was understandably skeptical of that response given the proximity of defendant's home. Further, the record does not shed light on how defendant's "urinary urgency" was met. The record contains no suggestion that during the prolonged series of events that followed his emergence from behind the trees — his questioning by the officer, the pat-down, the wait for the arrival of backup officers, the arrest, and the subsequent transportation of defendant to the police station — defendant acted in any way that he was prey to an importunate bladder. The void is only in the evidence. Nothing indicates that defendant's urgency was relieved or miraculously abated, simply nothing in the record to support the dissent's empathetic endorsement of defendant's defense based on the imminent nature of nature's call. Rather, it underscores the soundness of the conclusion of the majority, whose author's view is clearly untainted by the kind of personal feelings that are projected by the dissent. Defendant exhibited only a "weak excuse," not a weak bladder. Ante at (slip op. at _____).

Although amused by the opinions, the Chief Justice sensed in both of them a potential to undermine confidence in the Court. Sufficient time has passed that I feel it proper to report his suggestions to the two opinion writers. He wrote:

CONFIDENTIAL MEMORANDUM
TO: HONORABLE ROBERT L. CLIFFORD
HONORABLE ALAN B. HANDLER
FROM: CHIEF JUSTICE ROBERT N. WILENTZ
RE: My Funny Valentine
DATE: January 13, 1994

I hope that this note is not sent because of my jealousy about being excluded from the uproarious pissing debate. I am not at all convinced that what I am about to suggest is important, or, put differently, that the opinions in this matter, if they go out as presently written, will do no harm. They certainly will not do any great harm. So I'll just tell it to you the way it seems to me, and then you will do whatever you want to do.

It's fun for a court to have fun once in a while, even to have Justices whose style becomes fun. If it stays in-house, in New Jersey, in the Law Journal, and doesn't happen too often, it can add something to the Court. If it detracts, it detracts very little. My concern with this case is that [if] it is going to go beyond New Jersey, beyond the Law Journal, the legal propositions will be awash with the great humor that they have caused. I assume you both know that what is funny is not what you have said, but the fact that Justices have said it — the idea that a judge can talk about urine, bladders, piss, and actually argue about these fundamental needs is just more than most people can tolerate. It's positively amusing. Just what the case is all about will get very much lost, but the fact that Justices can disagree and really argue with each other about what it means to have to take a piss: ah, that's something that captures the imagination. It's the pissing Court. "Jersey Court in Pissing Contest." They'll certainly wait for our next opinion with more anticipation, and presumably, like all good comedians, we'll have to work hard to live up to our reputation.

If you are so inclined, I suggest that Justice Clifford note the credibility of defendant's story (with a straight face) and leave it at that. Justice Handler can fold his tent.

No big deal — if you want to leave it the way it is we'll all live through it. The point is simple. They will be laughing — at us.
R.N.W.

That was the end of the discussion. It was enough that the Chief should express his concern for the well-being of the Court that both members immediately withdrew their opinions.

The Chief Justice's comments on opinions could be brutally frank. In an opinion I had circulated concerning the right to trial by jury in a chancery case, I had written, "the right to trial by jury is an ever-present reminder of our belief in the importance of the individual." He responded, "C---. It's got nothing to do with that except in your mind. It is the importance of the community vs. the king."

His comments on circulating opinions were always helpful. He was a beautiful writer and a great reader. Even in his final illness, he offered valuable suggestions to me in connection with an opinion about a capital defendant's right to waive any further appeal. The case was *State v. Martini*. It had been argued on June 4, 1996, and I had circulated the draft opinion for the Court on June 13, writing:

> It is difficult to explain why a murderer who has admitted his guilt and had his conviction and sentence of death affirmed on direct appeal should not be granted his request to be executed immediately. For some no explanation is necessary. For others no explanation will suffice. For those who wish to understand we explain that under our form of government it is not the inmate on death row ... who determines when and whether the State shall execute a prisoner; the regular processes of the law make that determination.

The Chief Justice was at Mount Sinai Medical Center in New York City, but he sent back the draft, recommending that there be two concluding sentences in the paragraph instead of one and that the opinion recite simply, "The law itself makes that determination." "Not much better," he wrote, "but you pick it." He also suggested that I use a sentence from page four of the opinion that said that "[In *State v. Koedatich*] we found that the public has an interest in the reliability and integrity of a death sentencing decision that transcends the preferences of individual defendants." His suggestions made the opinion better but they saddened me, to think of him in the hospital and still working to the end. In another part of the opinion I had left an open question of "what to do about payment for the court's expert." He wrote in the margin. "Pay him (or her) — just figure out who gets the bill — don't go grey!" A small thing, but characteristic of his style: just do it.

Most of all, he knew when we needed to be prodded and when we needed to be praised. We all loved receiving compliments from him. My favorite came from a zoning case. He was never able to be completely flowery. In this case, he wrote, "OK, CJ. Dan: don't get mad, but I must tell you: You write clear, just like a great English judge. (At least when you're thinking.)"

Each of us valued words of respect from the Chief Justice. He was especially generous in support of our circulated opinions, always reading them carefully and commenting, in some cases, with humor.

On one occasion, the Chief had been working on an opinion, *Madden v. Township of Delran*, about the municipal obligation to provide indigent defendants with representation. The issue had provoked a simmering dispute. Controversial orders had been issued requiring counties to provide additional funds for court costs. The members of the Court exhibited a noticeable lack of enthusiasm toward the Chief Justice's first draft. Several justices suggested that its tone was "imperialistic, if not monarchical," in addition to being "autocratic." The Chief's covering letter to us with the revised opinion is an example of his humor:

As others have said with more conviction [a veiled reference to a prior member of the Court who dealt with suggestions for change in an opinion by ignoring them while graciously stating that all suggestions had been incorporated in the revised opinion], I have accepted all of your suggestions. There is a tone of friendship in the opinion that may have formerly been lacking. The question of power to compel municipalities to pay counsel is explicitly left open, although the possible sources of the power are mentioned. Some slight repetition has been eliminated, others retained. [The municipality] is flagged but not flogged. The question of whether we will do anything about [the municipality] is not addressed, but our power to [order the provision of] counsel is fairly clearly stated. Other suggestions, too numerous to mention, have been graciously incorporated in the revision. Some imperious observations ... have been eliminated. In deference to Justice Clifford, I have not added any *more* footnotes.

That kind of graciousness enlivened the tedious hours of Court conferences and defined his relationship with us.

At the same time, his work habits were unassailable. It was not uncommon for him to send us faxes well past midnight, even toward the end of his life. Three months before he died, I received a fax he had sent at 12:34 a.m. about an ethics case.

One of the Chief Justice's engaging qualities was his interest in our travel plans. In 1986, when my wife and I were planning a trip to Venice, he said, "Of course Dan, you must stay at the Cipriani." We did not stay there. It cost $600 a night. When we arrived at the Pension Seguso instead, we found a bottle of champagne and flowers in the room with the following message:

> Barbara and Dan,
> Just wanted to get you started right. You're on vacation, forget everything else, enjoy every minute of it. And eat something before you taste the wine.
> Love, Robert Wilentz

And when the Chief Justice went on vacation himself, he often kept in touch with the Court, as shown in this letter written on the stationery of the La Bastide de Gordes in Provence, in the south of France, on Sept. 7, 1994:

PHOTO COURTESY OF DANIEL J. O'HERN

Robert Wilentz, shown here in 1994 in Venasque, France, sent long memos to justices who were headed abroad for vacation. He gave advice on what they should see and sometimes surprised them with flowers and a bottle of champagne sent to their hotel rooms.

Mes Amis:

This was a lovely hotel. I have broken the little safe in the room (no great loss: the concierge (f.) told me that she had the key), the shower thing (the one that used to be attached to a metal tube), the beautiful window lock, lost my key to the room, paraded through the lobby in my shower robe on my way to the pool, and requested a drink in the hotel lounge at 11 PM — it closes at 7:30. In fact all of Gordes closed at 7:30. There are 2,021 permanent residents, all dead, and about 5,000 tourists, all German. The outstanding characteristics of the town (other than the urge to get out) are the extremely steep & narrow "walks," made from ankle-straining stones and the age of everything (500 yrs. — otherwise they tear it down).

Visited Venasque where there is not a suitable monument erected in honor of Justice and Mrs. O'Hern. A little trip he suggested for an evening ("The roads are all well marked") took 2 hours & but for my bravery, could have resulted in extreme panic. It takes 20 minutes with the benefit of light. I will never forget it — a little opinion on inverse capitalization & retroactive taxation of illegal tax foreclosure sales & proceeds will be appropriately assigned. Venasque supposedly has 785 residents including a handful whose families have lived there since the 7th century (B.C. or A.D. — it makes no difference); the rest are dead.

Leave tomorrow (by car) for Paris. All is well! C.J. (?)

P.S. — No word from anyone yet on the tomatoes!

The latter was a reference to one of his greatest undertakings — growing tomatoes at his home in Deal. As the Chief was about to return from his trip, Justice Clifford replied:

September Fourteenth, 1994
TO: Chief Justice Wilentz
FROM: RLC
RE: Stewardship

Well, Chief, I must confess that I am left wondering just what is the big deal about your job. I mean, this has been a piece of cake: a little conference in Morristown, a little argument time in Trenton, and nobody bothering me with nothin'. ... No probation officers picketing, no bar association [complaints] ..., no urgent communiqués (save for seventeen copies of your travel schedule, sent by [Steven] Bonville to each member's home and chambers, then faxed, then delivered by Charlie [Brill], then the whole process repeated every third day).

So on your return you will find your judicial machinery as finely-tuned and running as smoothly as when you left it. The only glitch I experienced came, as might be expected, from the conduct of some of the members, who as a lot remain incorrigible. Why, for instance, should the presiding justice be subjected, during oral argument, to the insolence of a member drawing the hand across his throat as a sign that he had heard quite enough from the poor disciplinary respondent who was struggling to avoid the three-years suspension that he richly deserves and will doubtless receive? Why must my every effort to bring order to our proceedings be met with indifference bordering on contempt? But you know these problems all too well, and I am sure Senior Associate-Justice-in-Waiting Handler will have to endure much of the same.

So, welcome back. And be prepared for close examination by some of your nosey colleagues on the identity of the persons with whom you [were traveling].

Tomato report to be delivered orally.

RLC

PHOTO BY DANIEL J. O'HERN

The gracious leadership exhibited by Robert Wilentz, shown here in 1993 celebrating Gary Stein's 60th birthday, led to respect for his goals. And that, Stein has said, "sometimes helped forge consensus where none seemed possible."

The Chief's witty personality drew the admiration and affection of the members of our Court.

The Chief Justice was a joy to be with. I often traveled with him to and from the New Jersey shore in bad weather. Invariably, we would stop after argument or conference at a tavern in South Trenton. Sometimes we would talk at the bar with other patrons, but never discuss the business of the Court. We sat with the Chief's driver, Charlie Brill. He was a bad influence on the Chief; he kept him supplied with cigarettes. Another stopping point for us was the Clarksburg Inn, a place of legend that opened in 1854 in western Monmouth County. On these occasions, the Chief always picked up the tab; I had the proverbial fishhooks in my pockets.

He had warm, personal relationships with the Court members. And it was reciprocal. After Jackie died in 1989, the Chief Justice fell ill, probably the result of neglect of his own health. As he was recuperating that summer, I offered to take him for a walk on the boardwalk in Ocean Grove. He expressed reluctance, uncomfortable about being seen in public in a less-than-robust state. I reassured him that no one would recognize him, and sure enough no one did — at least as far as we could tell.

Chief Justice Wilentz was a great conversationalist. I remember a night in the summer of 1991 during the Persian Gulf crisis. We were having our annual dinner at the Breakers in Spring Lake with Justice Marie L. Garibaldi and her mother, Marie, fondly known as "the General" for her strong personality. The General was condemning Iraqi President Saddam Hussein's invasion of Kuwait, and the Chief was playing devil's advocate. He defended Hussein's position as having been based on a line in the sand drawn by white men. It was all in good fun on the Chief's part.

One year, the Chief Justice asked whether he could bring his housekeeper, Araminta Mustafa, who had been chosen by his staff and was a great comfort to him. I told him it was fine, and so did Justice Garibaldi and the General. So she joined us, to the joy of the Chief.

The Chief Justice also was a great mimic. One example occurred during the post-argument discussion of a major commercial case. The lawyer was a rather famous television personality who grilled guest panelists on his show. The Chief did a hilarious imitation of counsel's argument, complete with a Groucho Marx strut around the conference table: "Chief Justice Wilentz, how can you say that about my client?"

The Chief Justice also took great interest in our families. On March 18, 1991, on the occasion of the wedding of our son Daniel, we received the following note:

Dear Barbara and Dan:

As I just told Dan, the wedding and reception were a joy to behold and a joy to attend. The newlyweds were bright, beaming and beautiful (and handsome), the wedding party a happy bubbling sight for elderly eyes, and the entire assemblage, including some dour judges, a marvelous assortment of fine elegant people, most of them happily young, and all of them happy. The church and the ceremony, to my unpracticed eye and ear, were perfect, the words of the priest, and the priest himself, so unpretentious, simple, yet full of meaning, and the celebration that followed so fulfilling in every way for everyone.

I have said too much already, so I won't compliment you on your selection of the day, the place, the food, the band, I'll just say when it was over I had the feeling that all is right with the world. You have a great family. Love, Robert

What kept the Chief on an even keel was that he was essentially a modest man. He never lost touch with his childhood roots in Perth Amboy. Throughout his life, he spent New Year's Eve with his boyhood friends in Perth Amboy. And he often recalled his involvement with his own family in the life of that community. Although he had a keen intellect, he was wise enough to know that the best of judges are not perfect. For instance, he was the first to acknowledge that we must often decide cases without precedent. In upholding Megan's Law in *Doe v. Poritz*, the sex-offender community-notification act, he wrote:

We sail on truly uncharted waters, for no other state has adopted such a far-reaching statute. All other notification statutes apparently make public notification discretionary on the part of officials; the statute before us, however, mandates it.

Another case that broke new ground was *Kelly v. Gwinnell*, the social-host decision.

Two years later, on Dec. 22, 1986, a news report on Monitor Radio, the broadcast service of *The Christian Science Monitor*, said a study showed that U.S. motorists' chances of being involved in a drunken driving accident were the lowest ever. Most experts said "the new mood of responsibility began to take shape" after the *Kelly* ruling, according to the broadcast. "The spirit of the *Kelly* decision has taken hold nationwide in the minds of legislators and the courts. Nine states have enacted dramshop laws in the last year and a half. In addition, 14 states have raised their legal drinking age to 21 and now all but eight states agree on a stiffer definition of legal drunkenness, a blood alcohol level of .1 percent or lower," the broadcast continued.

In a commentary published on Aug. 4, 1996, in *The Record* of Hackensack, Justice Gary S. Stein summarized best the Chief Justice's qualities of leadership:

If the Chief felt strongly about a specific case, he sometimes would elect to begin the discussion. On occasion, his opening views would be rejected by each of the six members who spoke after him. His self-confidence and open mindedness were never better illustrated than by those cases in which no one agreed with him, and the Chief would almost invariably reverse course and join the rest of the Court.

He always set high standards for the Court's deliberations. If once around the table did not produce a consensus, he would go around again, and then a third time. If any member wished to continue discussing a case, the Chief kept the floor open. If we were deadlocked about a result or a rationale, he would patiently prolong the debate while it remained productive, and then tactfully suggest that we revisit the issue the next time the Court convened. If a discussion got the least bit edgy, he would poke good-natured fun at someone or something to lighten the tone.

Many of Robert Wilentz's decisions covered new territory. One example was his opinion upholding Megan's Law, which he said reflected society's right to protect itself.

PHOTO BY BILL KOSTROUN

As we all did, he treasured our collegiality and believed that the Court eventually would reach consensus, no matter how difficult the issue. His goal
was justice, and he knew that that goal was best
achieved when the Court functioned in an atmosphere of free and open deliberation, characterized
by trust and candor.

When writing an opinion for the Court, the Chief
graciously accepted criticism and readily offered to
revise his own work to meet the concerns of various
members. Sometimes he feigned injury at the af-
front to his work, but in good humor he eventually
would agree to make the requested revisions.

His respect for the other members of the Court and
his natural facility for gracious leadership paid
rich dividends. In my 11··· years on the Court,
I never heard a single harsh word spoken at conference. The Court's collegiality was unique. And
on those important occasions when he cared pas-
sionately about an issue, he received the Court's
thoughtful attention. He had earned it. Whether or
not we agreed entirely with his views, the members' respect for his basic goals and commitment to
justice sometimes helped to forge consensus where
none seemed possible. Consistent with basic principle, individual members of the Court would try
to temper their views in order to advocate the common good. The congenial atmosphere the Chief had
fostered made compromise both possible and desir-
able. ...

His work ethic and his output were prodigious. For the Court to receive a 10-or 15-page, single-spaced memo from the Chief about a case, an opinion, or an administrative problem was commonplace. His memos were always direct, piercing, and provocative. Of course, we all worked hard, but the standard had been set.

On the last day of each term, when our work was virtually completed, the Chief would break out some fine champagne and we would sit around and reminisce about the term's highs and lows, trading insults and barbs, needling each member in turn and the Chief most of all. The glow generated by that annual event was not only from the champagne, but also from our warmth and affection for each other, for the institution on which we were privileged to serve, and for the man who calmly and graciously had steered us through the term.

During his funeral service in Perth Amboy, the Chief Justice was praised by former governors, and hundreds of people came to pay their respects. His children spoke of him as a father, as a great piano player, as a man who could dance around the living room floor at holiday time to *The Nutcracker Suite* and as a warm and loving friend. Their perspective was different from mine, but I could easily recognize the father they adored. Our Court has moved on, and it will continue to render justice for all, consistent with its great tradition. But the Court — and all the people of New Jersey — have good reason to look back with gratitude and pride on the 17-year tenure of Chief Justice Wilentz. We shall not soon see his like again. I was lucky to have served with him.

ILLUSTRATION COURTESY OF DANIEL J. O'HERN

Members of the Court relied on large paper charts during conferences to map out key arguments in a case. On one occasion, some justices and staff used the medium to let Robert Wilentz know their thoughts about the temperature in the building.

ILLUSTRATION BY THE RECORD OF HACKENSACK

The death in 1996 of Robert Wilentz, whose Court had handed down landmark rulings in matters from exclusionary zoning to the right to die, was keenly felt.

3
The Senior Justice

Justice Clifford was our senior member, a role little known but of importance to the life of the New Jersey Supreme Court. By custom and tradition, the senior justice runs the Court conferences, and calls the motion and certification petitions for vote. Justice Clifford conducted the conferences with skill and aplomb. Mixing cynicism, irony and flattery, he kept us in line, all the time feigning deference to Chief Justice Wilentz: "What would you like to do now, Chief?"

Justice Clifford was born in Passaic on Dec. 17, 1924. A graduate of Lehigh University in 1947 and Duke University School of Law in 1950, he arrived on the bench with a mixture of 20 years in private practice and three years in the cabinet of Gov.

William T. Cahill, in which he served as state commissioner of banking, insurance, and institutions and agencies.

His retirement on Dec. 17, 1994, marked the end of one of the longest and most distinguished careers in the Court's history. Since the adoption of the New Jersey

Constitution in 1947, only Justice Nathan L. Jacobs has sat longer. Justice Clifford served on the Court for 21 years with justices appointed by five governors, and retired at age 70 as mandated by the Constitution.

Justice Clifford wrote hundreds of opinions, including many priceless dissents. Many of his majority opinions are of enduring significance. These include *Murray v. Lawson* (restricting residential protests by pro-life groups); *T & E Industries, Inc. v. Safety Light Corporation* (permitting a property owner to assert a strict-liability action for abnormally dangerous activities against a predecessor in title); *Chavis v. Rowe* (determining that a judicial inquiry into removal of a church deacon from his post was prohibited by the First Amendment); and *Lawrence v. Bauer Publishing & Printing Ltd.* and *Kotlikoff v. The Community News* (upholding freedom of the press).

I was most proud to join his opinion in *Dewey v. R.J. Reynolds Tobacco Co.*, in which the Court held that the Federal Cigarette Labeling and Advertising Act did not pre-empt a state-court action based on New Jersey's product liability laws. The decision is firm in its restatement of the fundamental principles of federalism: until Congress, in the exercise of Commerce Clause powers, expressly displaces state law, states remain sovereign guarantors of the personal well-being of their citizens. Before Justice Clifford's reaffirmation of this principle, Professor Laurence Tribe of Harvard Law School had addressed this issue in "Federalism With Smoke and Mirrors," an article in the June 7, 1986, issue of *The Nation*. He found that the contrary view of pre-emption (that once Congress acts in a field of public regulation, it displaces the states) had "the burning force of a prairie fire, and it is hard to see what structures of state compensation would survive the ensuing conflagration."

PHOTO BY BILL KOSTROUN

Justice Robert Clifford's colleagues felt his command of the English language and his clarity greatly improved the Court's opinions.

The prairie fire died out for a time in no small measure because of the familiar clarity of mind that Justice Clifford displayed in all his work. Words meant not what he wanted them to mean but rather what they meant of themselves. He read the language of the Federal Cigarette Labeling and Advertising Act and knew that if Congress had wanted to pre-empt state law, it would have said so. He wrote:

> We are convinced that had Congress intended to immunize cigarette manufacturers from packaging, labeling, misrepresentation, and warning claims, it knew how to do so with unmistakable specificity.

I want primarily, however, to convey an understanding of Justice Clifford's contribution to the law as literature. His extraordinary command of the English language made all of our opinions better. In *State v. Heslop*, he wrote:

> Because part of the debate on the accuracy of the trial court's charge seems to have ripened into a disagreement on, of all things, correct grammar, I write separately only to take up the cudgels in defense of linguistic hygiene. I hasten to add that I approach the task with but the slenderest of credentials, particularly in the face of the sophisticated analyses spun out in my colleagues' opinions. My own primitive frame of reference is limited pretty much to what I learned around 1935-36 from Miss Doane in the sixth grade at Franklin School No. 3, Passaic, New Jersey. Miss Doane was not one to brook sloppy grammar.

He detested fakery and pettifoggery. In 1991, I wrote an opinion, from which Justice Clifford dissented, concerning the distribution of life insurance proceeds after divorce. I had quoted from a law review article noting the prevailing American rule that insurance proceeds are to be awarded to the former spouse when an insured has failed after divorce and remarriage to change a beneficiary designation. The article, "Life Insurance Beneficiaries and Divorce," 65 Tex. L. Rev. 635 (1987), concluded: "Many states' laws compel just such an inequitable result."

My opinion in the case, *Vasconi v. Guardian Life Insurance Company of America*, was returned from a first circulation to him with grammatical corrections and this derisive insertion to my argument: "As you might have guessed from the bogus way we phrased the issue," only one conclusion could follow.

His command of grammar is awesome. The *New Jersey Lawyer*, the New Jersey State Bar Association's weekly newspaper, once published an article that analyzed one of Justice Clifford's opinions. The authors of the article quoted from the opinion but added a comma to one of its sentences. Justice Clifford wrote the following letter to the authors:

February Fourth, 1994
Robert H. Bernstein, Esq.,
Michael T. Bissinger, Esq.,
Messrs. Grotta, Glassman & Hoffman
75 Livingston Avenue
Roseland, New Jersey
07068

Gentlemen:
Now look, you guys, I don't mind you criticizing the substance of my opinions, thumping my

jurisprudence, ripping my reasoning, or huffing and puffing at my analysis. I really don't. But when you start messing with my punctuation, WATCH OUT.

Your recent piece on Employee Drug Testing in the New Jersey Lawyer contains the following sentence:

The New Jersey Supreme Court affirmed the Appellate Division's holding "that Coastal Eagle's firing of Hennessey, an at-will employee in a safety sensitive position, as a result of his failing a random urine test[,] did not violate a clear mandate of public policy.

The gratuitous insertion of the bracketed comma after "test" is designed to point out to the reader that the opinion's author blew it; that the sentence *requires* a comma at that point; that any fool should have known as much; and that you, the authors, were perceptive enough to catch the glitch and are delighted to correct it.

WRONG! Trust me on this one; DEAD WRONG. NOT EVEN CLOSE. The use of a comma where you would include it is not a matter of choice, not optional, not maybe okay. It's INCORRECT. Why? Because it separates the subject from the verb, a major-league, Olympic NO-NO.

Ah well, at least someone was thinking about punctuation, which is more than most lawyers (and judges and newspaper reporters and columnists and teachers) do nowadays.

Otherwise, good article. Please, just keep your hooks off my punctuation.

Cordially,
/s/ Robert L. Clifford

Justice Clifford especially loathed the use of footnotes in opinions and he did not hesitate to make this clear to us. In one case, I had written an opinion containing only two footnotes. One particularly offended him. This gave him the opportunity for the retort, in *In re Opinion 662*, which left us all fearful of even a single footnote:

> In fact, I deplore resort to footnotes not only in this case in particular but in judicial opinions generally. They distract. They cause the reader to drop the eyes; to absorb what is usually a monumental piece of irrelevancy or pseudo-scholarship but is sometimes — as here — a significant pronouncement that rightly belongs in the text; and then to return, without skipping a beat, to the point of departure on the upper part of the page. The whole irritating process points up the soundness of John Barrymore's observation that "[reading footnotes is] like having to run downstairs to answer the doorbell during the first night of the honeymoon," *quoted in* Norrie Epstein, *The Friendly Shakespeare* 75 (1992).

And so the footnote in the Court's opinion represents yet another setback in my woefully-ineffectual campaign to abolish footnotes from our opinions.

PHOTO BY BARBARA O'HERN

Members of the Court and their families gathered in 1993 for Gary Stein's 60th birthday. Shown from left: Robert Clifford, who joined Stein on a 60-mile bicycle ride to mark the occasion; Et Stein, the justice's wife; and Daniel O'Hern.

Justice Clifford was as generous with others as with me. Through the years, Supreme Court clerks became familiar with his writing style. Once, in an end-of-term bit of humor, some clerks circulated a mock opinion that purports to discipline fellow clerks for taking an unauthorized holiday. Attached to the opinion was an "edit-it-yourself kit," condensing some of Justice Clifford's most favored editorial changes. Somehow, this mock opinion fell into the hands of Justice Clifford. He relentlessly disabused the clerks of the thought that they had learned anything about the English language or about writing style in the course of their year with the Court.

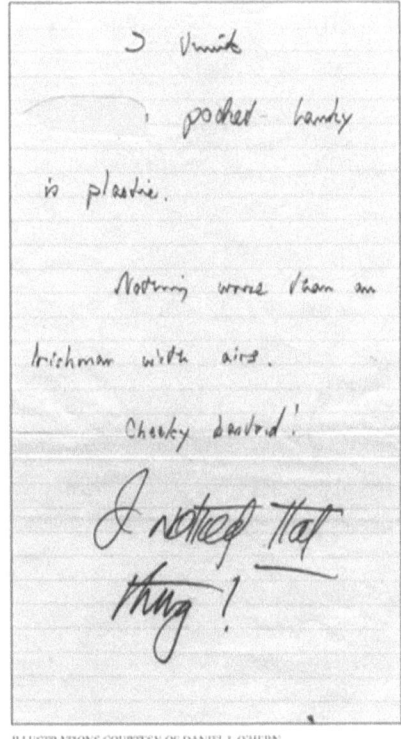
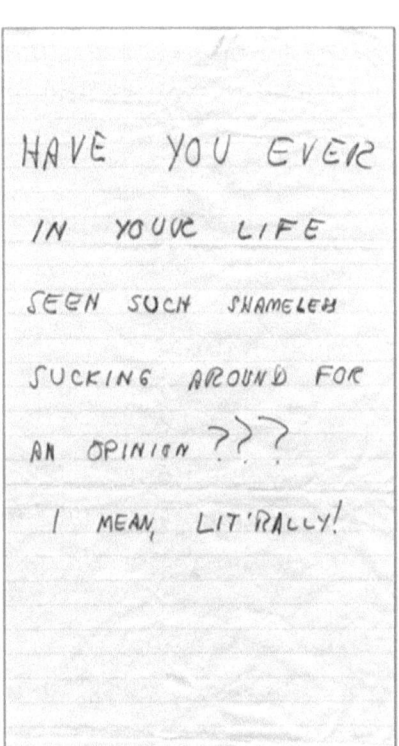

ILLUSTRATIONS COURTESY OF DANIEL J. O'HERN

From time to time, Robert Clifford was moved to slide notes to Daniel O'Hern during oral argument. At left, he remarked on the attire of one attorney: "I think [name of attorney deleted]'s pocket-hanky is plastic. Nothing worse than an Irishman with airs. Cheeky bastard!" O'Hern responded: "I noticed that thing!" At right, Clifford commented on the impact of one attorney's approach to winning over the justices.

Justice Clifford once tired of this effort. On Dec. 30, 1992, having decided to resign from his role as Court grammarian, he circulated the following holiday verse:

FOR IMMEDIATE ATTENTION

'Twas the week after Christmas,
And through these dimmed halls
Echoed moanings and groanings
That bounced off the walls.

At his desk, all bent over,
A figure appeared,
It was not old St. Nick
'Though it did have a beard.

He carried no sack,
No toy, no utensil,
But an old dog-eared Blue Book
And a sharpened red pencil.

He sat at the desk
And flipped through opinions,
Demanding a cite check
From one of his minions.

The pages they flew
And the hours went by,
The courthouse was hushed,
For darkness was nigh.

But at his dull labors
Old Bob still persisted,
Crying out as he worked:
"These cites are all twisted!"

"The grammar's atrocious.
I'm losing the game;
I'm giving it up,
Send it back whence it came."

And so girl and boys,
With this feeble endeavor
I relinquish my duties
And red pen forever.

No more will your sec'ys
Cringe when they see
A returned draft opinion
From old RLC.

The old guy has had it,
The work is too much;
You're all on your own with
"Accord," "see," and such.

No hyphens, no "cf."s,
No "that," "which," and "when."
Just one last request:
will you Bronze my red pen?

Fortunately for all of us, he had a change of heart and continued to red-pencil opinions until his retirement.

Justice Clifford was restrained in his appraisal of my own opinions. I often exhibited a hand-wringing style of writing that would conclude with a rhetorical question intended to suggest to the reader how difficult the issues were to resolve. He took particular delight in chiding me whenever I used this approach. He thought this a dreadful breach of opinion-writing style. To illustrate his point, on one occasion he sent me a birthday card that was a parody of my writing style. The card read:

> Would we not want to wish you many happy
>   returns?
> We have struggled in vain to conquer old age, but
>   who among us would admit defeat?
> How, then, can we handle this? What do we say to
>   creeping senility?
> We poor mortals are ill-equipped to deal with
>   these age-old problems. But is not the door
>   always open???

His reports on conferences conducted in the Chief Justice's absence were priceless. Here is one:

January Twenty-Seventh, 1993
TO: Chief Justice Wilentz
FROM: Your Stand-in
RE: Court Conference in Morristown on January Twenty-Sixth, 1993

Herewith my report on the Morristown conference.

Two preliminary observations are in order: (a) The members much enjoy the respite from multi-page single-space memos on all manner of earthshaking subjects, but they are fearful of the paper flood that will accompany your return. They wish me to express their collective hope that you will treat your staff, your office communication machines, and your colleagues with mercy and forbearance next week. And the week thereafter. Just *tell* us what's on your mind; don't make us read it. (b) A minor personal note: when I go to the National Conference nobody knows from nothin'; when the Chief Justice goes, [*Star-Ledger* reporter Herb] Jaffe tags along and devotes barrels of ink to such cosmic observations as "I can't talk about that because maybe we'll get a case on it some day." *Star-Ledger* 1-27-93. Oh, well.

Now to the business.

1. The luncheon menu (this is business?) consisted of a hearty, thick pea soup, with gingerbread, whipped cream, and applesauce for dessert. All home cooked, of course, including the croutons for the soup. Lavish praise for the chef.

2. The assignment of cases went as follows, in the order as they appear on the worksheet:

● ● ●

(f) A-71 *Hopkins v. Fox and Lazo* Alan will write to affirm. The vote is five to two, but once again we are shaky. I think you, Alan, and I believe that Sylvia [Pressler] has this one close to the mark.

I agree with Alan that we should forget the Restatement formulation of liability, and I agree with Alan that we should eschew the traditional labels that we trot out to address trespasser, social guest, and business-invitee cases. Dan wants to affirm on the narrowest possible grounds, maybe limiting the conditions that would give rise to liability to his "missing brick" example at oral argument.

Gary has trouble with the duty to inspect. He points out that the Appellate Division does not touch the question of whether the broker was negligent in not discovering the alleged defect; and he sees the question as whether an objectively-reasonable broker should discover the condition and appreciate its dangerous nature. Marie and Stew think we are full of soup. What Neanderthals!

The foregoing synopses are bare-bone. They do not pretend adequately to set forth the views of the members. But hey, look at it this way: when Alan assumes this lofty perch in a mere twenty-two months and twenty-one days, your reading of his report will take a week and you'll spend another week figuring out what he said!

One might think from the above that I enjoyed a modicum of success in getting through the ministerial business of running the calendar. Little did I know the disaster that awaited on the administrative stuff. How do you stand these people? I cannot

bear to tell you any more than that your suggestion for immediate revision of the EFC [Ethics
Financial Committee] rules was roundly — but I
mean *roundly* — rejected. Far be it from me to tat-
tle, but Justice Garibaldi persuaded us all to ignore
your recommendation. Justice Handler insisted
that we ignore it. Justice O'Hern wishes that we
do whatever it is we are going to do "tastefully";
and Justice Stein, with what he perceives (hallu-
cinates) as a dose of "practicality," allowed as how
the EFC cannot do much to hurt us now. We did not
hear from the centrist — or at least I do not recall
his leadership role. The upshot seemed to be that
we can wait until the Michels Committee issues its
report before we go your route.

Look, don't blame me, I just work here. Likewise
in respect of your thoughtful suggestion on *In re
Opinion 26* [concerning real estate closing prac-
tices] the hostility that your recommendation en-
gendered is so embarrassing that I cannot recount
the members' reactions in detail.

Shaken, I asked that it be held for February
First or Second so that "those people" could screech
at you instead of me. (They cannot pay you enough
for this crummy job.)

We all hope that you enjoyed a long rest, paid attention to your diet, and that your too-brief separation
from your colleagues, painful as you may have found

it, will produce a congenial and indulgent attitude in the face of our manifold shortcomings on your return.

Clifford, J., King for a Week

In addition to having a great mind, Justice Clifford has a great personality. A slight sense of that can be gleaned from a remark I overheard during Gov. Florio's inauguration on Jan. 18, 1990. After the ceremony, Chief Justice Wilentz, knowing that Justice Clifford was a piano player, asked Justice Clifford what he thought of a composition done for the occasion by Florio's son. Justice Clifford replied: "He has a remarkable facility for orchestration. He used all the instruments. It reminded me of Berlioz."

PHOTO BY STEPHEN N. TOWNSEND

Current and former members gathered in December 1994 to mark Robert Clifford's retirement. Shown left to right are Sidney Schreiber, Robert Wilentz, Daniel O'Hern, Clifford, Alan Handler, Stewart Pollock, Marie Garibaldi, James Coleman Jr., Gary Stein and Morris Pashman.

"*I'll assume, then, my remarks have hit a responsive chord?*"

• •

CHIEF JUSTICE ANNOUNCES PERMANENT
NON-FUNCTIONING OF AIR CONDITIONING
IN HIS CHAMBERS AND
SUPREME COURT
CONFERENCE ROOM

Robert Wilentz liked to keep the Court quite cold, to the dismay of some colleagues and staff. That prompted Robert Clifford to substitute his own wording under a New Yorker cartoon in anticipation of the reaction to a breakdown of the air-conditioning system.

He was equally well-versed in baseball lore. During one conference, we were discussing *Scafidi v. Seiler*, a case dealing with the enhanced risk of injury flowing from a physician's failure to diagnose a disease in its early stages. Justice Clifford had written *Evers v. Dollinger*, a prior case dealing with the lost chance of recovery because of delayed diagnosis, and thought that case stated the law and need not be revised. He said, "I would not tinker with *Evers*; that imposes too much chance." Only a real baseball fan would catch his allusion to the famous double-play combination of the 1908 Chicago Cubs — Tinker to Evers to Chance.

His playfulness spilled over into our daily routines. I have a theory of life: deep inside everyone is a little child. Justice Clifford would throw paper-clip airplanes at me when I snoozed at conference. I am a low-energy guy and had a fear of falling asleep on the bench, though I never did.

I was forever boring the Court with clichés from my earlier life. One, drawn from my experience in the U.S. Navy of seeing crews routinely replaced even in mid-cruise, was that there is no such thing as an indispensable person.

Justice Clifford was as close to an indispensable person as we had. He was indispensable to the life of the Court, not just for his good humor and piercing wit, but for his enduring contributions to the style and substance of its work. Who among us could dissect a musical composition, dispense a metaphor drawn from baseball and douse a prairie fire of doctrinal error?

4
Stretch or Mandrake

This is what we called him. The Stretch reference is to Justice Handler's modest height; the Mandrake reference is to a popular comic-strip magician of the 1930s, Mandrake the Magician. We said Justice Handler could always conjure up the right result.

But Justice Handler had a richer role on our Court. Every great court needs a clean-up hitter, someone strong, someone certain, someone on whom others can rely to come through at crucial moments. That was Justice Handler's role. Of all the justices, he had the deepest mind, the greatest reservoir of judicial experience and understanding.

Justice Handler was born in Newark on July 20, 1931. He graduated with an A.B. degree, Phi Beta Kappa, in 1953 from Princeton University's Woodrow Wilson School of Public and International Affairs. After obtaining an LL.B. degree from Harvard Law School in 1956, he entered private practice in Newark.

In a tribute published in the Rutgers Law Journal in the spring of 2000, Justice Clifford described him as follows:

You won't believe it, but this is a very funny man. Not thigh-thumping, loud-mouthed, yuk-yuk hilarity. Just slow-to-sink-in, subtle, ironic, real funny stuff, delivered with a wry little smile and all the voice inflection of an undertaker closing a deal with the bereaved. The listener must pay close attention. You will have to take the foregoing on faith — I cannot dredge up any examples, and besides the written word is simply not up to the task.

What you do *not* have to take on faith, and what any Court-watcher knows full well, is that when the topography of New Jersey jurisprudence in the second half of the 20th century is finally mapped out, Justice Handler's contributions will stand high. Every decision he made as a trial judge, a judge of the Appellate Division, and a justice of the Supreme Court bore his unmistakable stamp of careful analysis and precision of thought. My own view is that Alan Handler is one of maybe four honest-to-goodness, gold-plated, legitimate intellectuals to serve on the Court since the 1947 Constitution — the other three being Joseph Weintraub, Nathan Jacobs and Robert Wilentz. (There, I've done it — offended a couple of dozen other people, all of whom, I hasten to suggest, are or were extraordinarily bright, talented, even gifted. But the four I have named seem to me to be on a different plane. Comparisons such as the one I make here are probably unwise, even odious, but I feel pretty secure in announcing my appraisal of the Court's Cerebral Cases.)

Alan Handler the man is something else again. He's a bit of a mystery. Did any of us know that he played the flute? Rumor has it that he has taken up painting. He enjoys expertise at shoveling sheep dung out of barns. He dislikes travel. He follows professional football closely.

He is tenacious. Oh my is he tenacious! The titanic struggles between him and Justice Schreiber over who-knows-what point of law were great spectator sport: exposition, "but Sidney," exposition, "but Alan," exposition, "but Sidney," ad nauseam, until the Chief Justice mercifully stepped in before the rest of us fell off our chairs in boredom.

I have often thought that as a Supreme Court justice, Alan Handler was doing exactly what our Creator must have intended for him to do, and was doing it superbly. He was a judge from the top of his head to the tip of his toes.

When he retired in 1999, Justice Handler had served longer on the New Jersey Supreme Court than any other member but two, Justices Jacobs and Clifford.

Justice Handler's career paralleled that of Justice Jacobs. Each was a native of the Newark area. Each was a graduate of Harvard Law School. The careers of each spanned the two great transformative eras of the New Jersey Supreme Court. Established by the New Jersey Constitution of 1947, the Court set as its first task the reformation of common law to make it more consistent with the needs of post-World War II society, and more consistent with our understanding of the importance of the individual in that new society. Insurance law was reformed to provide that individuals who read an insurance policy would not be deprived of their fair understanding of the policy. Consumers who bought defective products would be able to gain recourse from the manufacturers.

Debtors who were led into unfair bargaining relationships were permitted to be relieved from the holder-in-due-course rule.

Toward the end of that period of change, the Court turned its attention to consideration of human rights, most notably in the context of equal access to housing and educational opportunity. In *Robinson v. Cahill*, the Court held that equal funding must be provided for children in disadvantaged communities. In *Oakwood at Madison, Inc. v. Township of Madison*, the Court held that New Jersey's zoning power must be exercised in the public interest to afford a fair opportunity for people of low and moderate income to live in every community.

Justice Handler was an active member of the New Jersey legal community during those years of change. Admitted to the bar in 1956, he joined the Office of the New Jersey Attorney General in 1961 and participated in many of those major changes in post-war society. In 1967, he was appointed to the Superior Court and in 1973 to the Appellate Division. He left the Appellate Division to serve as chief counsel to Gov. Byrne. In that capacity, he was involved in the reform of government funding. In 1977, Gov. Byrne appointed him to the New Jersey Supreme Court.

In an article, "Individual Worth," 17 Hofstra L. Rev. 493 (1989), Justice Handler wrote:

A surprising number of intense human dramas have recently played on the judicial stage. In the guise of court decisions, they have presented very poignant themes involving the most sensitive kinds of personal concerns — procreation, birth, health, survival and dying. What seems unusual about all of this is not the drama of these episodes but that they have been produced and directed by courts.

PHOTO BY BILL KOSTROUN

The concept of individual worth permeates Alan Handler's view of the judicial universe.

PHOTO BY NEW JERSEY SUPREME COURT

The other members of the Court looked to Alan Handler as a repository of judicial experience and wisdom. Shown here, clockwise from center, during a conference on Jan. 17, 1991, are Robert Wilentz, Handler, Daniel O'Hern, Gary Stein, Marie Garibaldi, Stewart Pollock and Robert Clifford.

For 22 years, Justice Handler was at center stage as these dramas unfolded. During that time, the New Jersey Supreme Court was called on to appraise the value of human life in wrongful birth and wrongful life claims, and Justice Handler cast his imprint on those decisions. His dissent in *Hummel v. Reiss* traced the long evolution of that doctrine and his role in shaping it. He wrote: "[T]he problem of valuing life against non-existence has perplexed the Court." *Hummel* concerned the rights of a severely disabled child, born before *Roe v. Wade*, to sue her mother's doctors and hospital for not respecting her mother's choice to undergo a therapeutic abortion. He explained how, in *Berman v. Allan*, the Court had come to recognize a cause of action for wrongful birth that had not been recognized in the seminal case of *Gleitman v. Cosgrove*. A wrongful birth action, as opposed to a wrongful life action, allowed parents who had been denied the right to choose to abort a child, to recover extraordinary expenses associated with the child's birth defect. Justice Handler recalled that his dissent in *Berman* had elaborated on the character of the tort: "The duty the physicians owed [to the mother] enveloped a duty to the unborn child. The breach of that duty affects both." He invoked the words of Justice Stewart G. Pollock, who wrote in *Schroeder v. Perkel*, "A family is woven of the fibers of life; if one strand is damaged, the whole structure may suffer. The filaments of family life, although individually spun, create a web of interconnected legal interests."

Finally, Justice Handler recalled that in *Procanik v. Cillo*, the Court had extended the web of familial protection to cover claims brought directly by handicapped children for extraordinary medical expenses. "When a child requires extraordinary medical care, the financial impact is felt not just by the parents but also by the injured child," the Court wrote. He thus reasoned that the denial of recovery to Kelly Hummel, because the malpractice had occurred before *Roe v. Wade*, was a "triumph of logic over justice."

Justice Handler's description of law as drama is like Justice Pollock's description of law as art in "The Art of Judging," 71 N.Y.U. L. Rev. 591 (1996). Each of these justices saw the relationship between law and the larger themes that govern our lives.

The theme of individual worth permeates Justice Handler's view of the judicial universe. In his memorable dissent in *State v. Marshall*, he noted "the emergence of the disquieting truth that capital punishment cannot really be made to work in a civilized society." He quoted the poet John Donne to remind us that we are all members of the same human family: "[A]ny man's death diminishes me, because I am involved in mankind; and therefore never send to know for whom the bell tolls; it tolls for thee." In *State v. Timmendequas*, he recalled François de La Rochefoucauld's maxim that death, like the sun, cannot be looked at steadily. Justice Handler wrote:

> The Court, in its attempt to look directly at death, loses its vision. ....The sacrifice we make when we sentence a defendant to life imprisonment instead of death pales in comparison to what we gain by holding that a defendant who cannot receive a fair trial in this State simply cannot be put to death, no matter how certain and clear his guilt. By abandoning principle and yielding judicial integrity in order to put the defendant to death, we lose, with even greater finality, the essence of fairness that is the heart of our criminal justice system.

Justice Handler believed that because judges lacked the authority to enforce their opinions through the use of force, the authority of the courts depended entirely on the public's acceptance of their opinions. To gain acceptance, a court's opinions must be "intrinsically persuasive," he wrote in "Jurisprudence and Prudential Justice," 16 Seton Hall L. Rev. 571 (1986). He explained:

[A] valid judicial decision is one that holds no secrets or hidden meanings, that inspires confidence that it is right as well as correct, sound as well as accurate, complete as well as pointed, fair as well as wise, and tolerant as well as decisive. It should reflect a sense of justice that is, in a word, prudential.

Because Justice Handler possessed that prudential sense of justice, the Court asked him to write *Abbott v. Burke* IV and V, among the most momentous of its decisions. He explained why it was that the Court would insist on the fulfillment of its mandate that equal educational opportunity be afforded to underprivileged children in inner-city schools. Although his writing style may have lacked the fervor of Chief Justice Wilentz's, it contained the same measure of commitment. Justice Handler wrote in *Abbott* IV:

The remedial proceedings to be conducted on remand are a step in the remedial process that should lead ultimately to the full realization of the constitutional educational opportunity. Although it remains our hope that needed comprehensive relief eventually will come from those branches of government more suited to the task, there can be no responsible dissent from the position that the Court has the constitutional obligation to do what it can to effectuate and vindicate the constitutional rights of the school children in the poverty-stricken urban districts.

Returning to the metaphor of law as art, Justice Handler may be viewed as an architect framing the structure of government. He is not a man of absolutes. He tended to view constitutional doctrine as having "play in the joints." In *Marsa v. Wernik*, Justice Handler held that having a particular town council member call for a silent meditation or deliver an invocation, the content of which was selected by the council member, did not violate the Establishment Clause. In *Knight v. City of Margate*, he found a "twilight zone" in the doctrine of separation of powers to enable the Court to sustain a delicate balance between the executive and legislative branches. He wrote:

> The constitutional doctrine of the separation of powers denotes not only independence but also interdependence among the branches of government. Indeed, the division of governmental powers implants a symbiotic relationship between the separate governmental parts so that the governmental organism will not only survive but will flourish.

In *State v. Schmid*, he found that a private property right had to yield to a broader need for free speech on a university campus. Conversely, in *New Jersey State Chamber of Commerce v. New Jersey Election Law Enforcement Commission*, he wrote to sustain the constitutionality of

New Jersey's election-funding laws despite some restraint on speech. In *Holmdel Builders Association v. Township of Holmdel*, he parsed the relationship between home rule and exclusionary zoning, and a state mandate for inclusionary zoning.

And he was every bit the common-law judge. Writing opinions for the Court in a vast array of contexts, he argued for the presumption that consumers of products would heed a warning, if given, in *Coffman v. Keene Corporation*; for the duty of a manufacturer to foresee alterations in its product, in *Brown v. U.S. Stove Company*; and for the duty of a commercial owner of property to provide a safe place of access for customers, in *Hopkins v. Fox & Lazo Realtors*. In all of those common-law cases, he displayed the skill of Benjamin Cardozo in weaving varied strands of doctrine to make the fabric of the law. (Justice Handler may not recall this, but when he circulated his opinion in *People Express Airlines, Inc. v. Consolidated Rail Corporation*, I wrote him a note expressing the view that the opinion would be as well remembered as *Palsgraf v. Long Island Railroad Company*.) In *People Express*, Justice Handler discarded the "physical harm" requirement for negligently inflicted economic losses and sustained a cause of action for foreseeable economic damages occasioned by a negligent act. He explained that many courts had based their refusal to allow recovery for purely economic losses on the "physical harm" requirement. Courts feared that if even one deserving plaintiff suffering solely economic damage were allowed to recover, all such plaintiffs could recover.

PHOTO BY RUTGERS UNIVERSITY

Alan Handler left his mark on a wide range of areas, particularly in cases that appraised the value of human life. He is shown here on April 5, 1984, when Rutgers University School of Law in Newark celebrated its 75th anniversary and saluted U.S. Supreme Court Justice William Brennan Jr., a former member of the New Jersey Supreme Court. Shown from left are Worrall Mountain, a former justice; Daniel O'Hern; Stewart Pollock; Brennan; Marie Garibaldi; Robert Clifford; Handler; Robert Wilentz and Morris Pashman, a former justice.

Justice Handler, however, believed that the Court could fashion a rule that limited liability, yet permitted adjudication of meritorious claims. In tracing the various exceptions to the "physical harm" requirement, he discovered a common theme: "When the plaintiffs are reasonably foreseeable, the injury is directly and proximately caused by defendant's negligence, and liability can be limited fairly, courts have endeavored to create exceptions to allow recovery." Thus, he concluded that "a defendant owes a duty of care to take reasonable measures to avoid the risk of causing economic damages, aside from physical injury, to particular plaintiffs or plaintiffs comprising an identifiable class with respect to whom defendant knows or has reason to know are likely to suffer from its conduct."

Finally, he was a righteous judge. In matters of attorney ethics, he demanded the highest qualities of character. In *In re Rigolosi*, he wrote to disbar an attorney despite a jury verdict that had exonerated him of witness tampering. More was required, he found, than that an attorney escape criminal conviction. He wrote: "Respondent's conduct reveals a flaw running so deep that he can never again be permitted to practice law. This is not a case of a novice who had not yet had opportunity to develop a sense of ethics. Respondent was an attorney steeped in the ways of law, government, and politics. No amount of good works can save someone who, with all the knowledge and experience that he accumulated, 'poisons the well of justice.'"

Alan Handler's decisions during his 32 years as a jurist on the trial, appellate and Supreme Court benches bore his stamp of careful analysis and precision of thought.

PHOTO BY CARMEN NATALE

In *In re McLaughlin*, Justice Handler discussed the need for attorneys and bar applicants to adhere to the highest principles of integrity. He explained:

> Candidates for the bar are expected to understand and satisfy the personal, educational, and professional requisites that inhere in good character and fitness and are indispensable in one seeking authorization to engage in the practice of law. Good character does not emerge on licensure. It is absurd to suggest that good character is not revealed until one becomes an attorney. The fundamental character traits of honesty and truthfulness are not valued in the abstract, but are assumed to be inherent aspects of one's personality; they can, and must, be considered the measure of a candidate's eligibility to seek admission to practice law and ability to fulfill the responsibilities of the legal profession.

Justice Handler was not a dreamer. He knew that much of a judge's work is routine. During his last conference with us in July 1999, he reflected that "my career ended with the case of a decayed grasshopper." The petition for certification had asked us to review a claim of spoliation of evidence.

His humor enlivened many conferences and hours between oral argument. Although he always managed, in a long series of Court portraits, to be photographed with a frown, Justice Handler had the lightest of hearts. He was the justice best able to tweak the imperialism of Chief Justice Wilentz. The Chief was the master of long, single-spaced letters as a means of conveying his views on matters of Court business. Of one such letter, Justice Handler said to the Chief Justice during a conference, "like any piece of good literature, upon a re-reading, you can always find new riches in your memos."

On another occasion, he satirized the Chief Justice's writing style in his 51-page ruling in the *Baby M* case by circulating a miniature version of the decision on eight pages about the size of bubble-gum cards.

During oral argument, Justice Handler's deep voice and slightly forbidding appearance made it impossible for lawyers to realize that he was often on their side. He would throw out rhetorical lifelines to lawyers who were adrift. Invariably, the lawyers would reject the lifeline, suspecting some ulterior motive on Justice Handler's part rather than a genuine desire to assist.

Justice Handler was my oldest friend on the Court. We had known each other at the bar for almost 40 years. I served with him on the Court every day for 18 years. He was a source of strength for all of us, a repository of accumulated wisdom with an innate ethical sense and a passion for justice best exemplified by his dissents in capital cases. When he retired, a headline in the *New Jersey Lawyer* on June 7, 1999, described him as "a key in Court's golden era."

5

Grover

Justice Pollock was the celebrity member of the New Jersey Supreme Court.

A member once called him Grover, an allusion to the legendary Grover Whalen, New York City's official greeter. I often had the opportunity to represent the Court at conferences of state chief justices and at other national events. During those gatherings, I would invariably be greeted, not with a question about how I felt or a comment about my opinions, but with this inquiry: "How is Stewart Pollock? Please give him my regards." This would be followed by effusive commentary on Justice Pollock's appearance, talents, humor and so forth. After a time, this began to grate on me. It was like hearing my mother-in-law describe to me her grandchildren other than my children. I learned to grit my teeth and smile.

Justice Clifford gave this portrait of him in a tribute in the Rutgers Law Journal in the spring of 2000:

> To say that his interests are varied seriously understates the case. Justice Pollock's enthusiasms zoom off in all directions.

He is an avid follower of the fortunes — and, alas, frequent on-field and off-field misfortunes — of a thoroughly mediocre outfielder whom the Mets acquired as excess baggage in a trade with the Houston Astros.

He knows, and with no prompting will tell you, a lot about cows. (If he is your passenger, avoid driving by pastures: they take him back to his days of operating a milk truck while he was working his way through Hamilton College. Hence the "cow" stories.)

He is a history buff—the history of anything. He has an insatiable appetite for books on the Revolution and the Civil War. He is fascinated by those guys who run around in funny uniforms and carry muskets while reenacting battlefield engagements.

Now he is into antique furniture. (Woe to the dealer who enters into serious price negotiations with Stewart Pollock: he'll learn a thing or two about thrift. Parsimony. Hard bargaining.)

He is an accomplished tennis player. (I leave it at that, for fear of animating Justice Stein's competitive instincts: he thinks he can beat Justice Pollock, and I'm not telling which one my money is on.)

His romance with his wife, Penny, is ongoing, nonstop, never ending.

PHOTO BY CARMEN NATALE

Stewart Pollock was generally described as the leading advocate of state constitutions as independent sources of guaranteed rights.

In the hierarchy of his affections a baseball signed by Nolan Ryan is a distant second to his wife and family. He has trouble sitting still. Standing still, too. Even at rest he is doing stretching exercises.

On the Court Justice Pollock's positions were always well thought-out. His recitations were direct, clear, concise, and his written opinions were the same. He had some interests that I thought a trifle off-beat — I mean, how can you build up a head of steam about the Uniform Commercial Code? — but he pursued them with admirable tenacity and resourcefulness, bugging the professors who taught that stuff, reaching out for the reporters of the restatements.

I notice that the professional journals have dubbed him, in post-retirement appraisals, the great "consensus builder." If that means that Justice Pollock sought to persuade others to agree with his point of view, that's baloney. He would state his view, and if you agreed with it, fine, and if you didn't, that was fine too. I cannot recall his ever engaging in proselytizing. What frequently happened, however, is that without any urging on the part of the author, others would be drawn to the logic and analysis of Justice Pollock's opinion and would alter or completely abandon their original views and adopt his.

He has come in recent years to fancy bow ties. Now that he is retired, he remembers to carry his wallet. He took up wind-surfing when he was close to sixty. He is tone deaf, a circumstance that does not discourage one whit his lusty, if painful, efforts at song. I am reliably informed that he is now learning to play golf.

Be forewarned: Fore!!

Justice Pollock was born in East Orange on Dec. 21, 1932. He graduated in 1954 from Hamilton College and in 1957 from New York University School of Law, where he was a Root-Tilden scholar. Root-Tilden scholars have been the cream of American legal society. Needy and deserving students were drawn to New York University from all over the country. He earned a master of laws degree from the University of Virginia in 1988, nearly a decade after his appointment to the Court. Justice Pollock began his legal career in 1958 as an assistant U.S. attorney in Newark and in 1960 went into private practice in Morristown. In 1974, he re-entered public service as a commissioner of the Board of Public Utilities and two years later became a member of the State Commission of Investigation. Justice Pollock served as chief counsel to Gov. Byrne in 1978 and 1979, when Byrne nominated him to the Supreme Court. Justice Pollock took his oath on June 28, 1979, and remained on the bench for 20 years.

His renown was richly deserved. Of all the members of our Court, Justice Pollock has had the greatest national impact. He was generally described as the leading national advocate of state constitutions as independent sources of guaranteed rights and set forth that thesis in his 1983 Weintraub Lecture, "State Constitutions as Separate Sources of Fundamental Rights," 35 Rutgers L. Rev. 707. Such a view of state constitutions has been considered the single most important development in American jurisprudence in the second half of the 20th century.

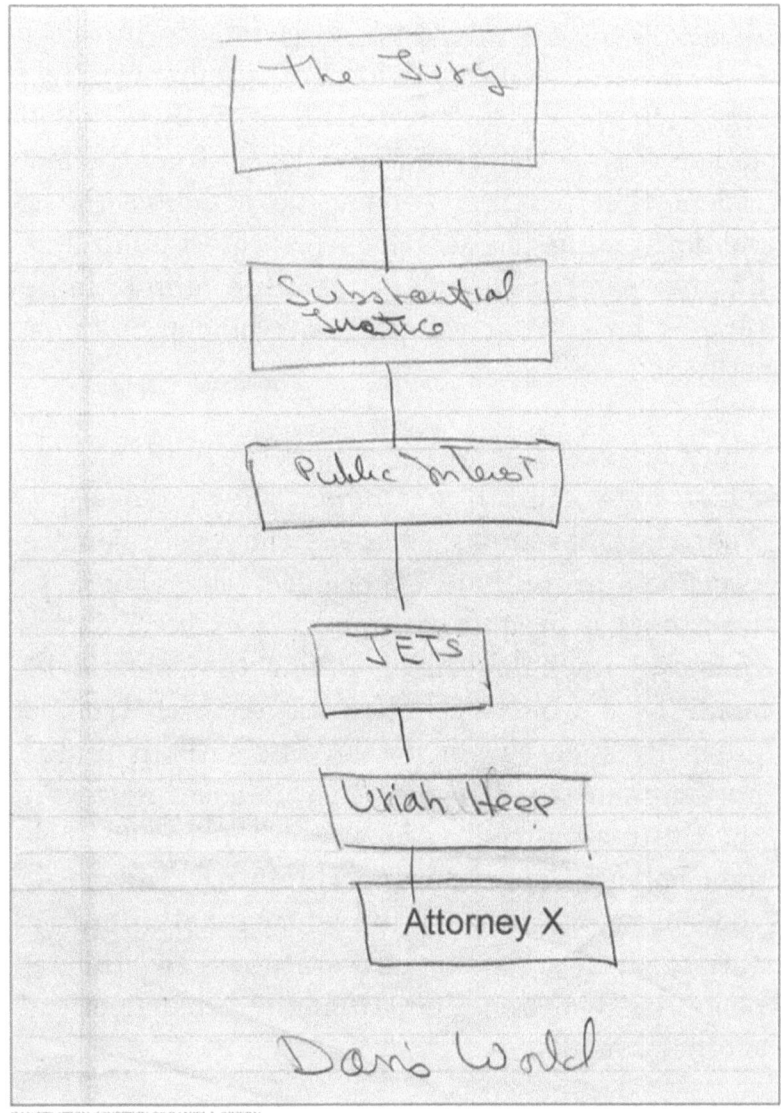

ILLUSTRATION COURTESY OF DANIEL J. O'HERN

Stewart Pollock drew this sketch of Daniel O'Hern's judicial icons and other interests after an attorney, whose name has been redacted, did not impress the Court.

Justice Pollock's interest and leadership in this field was the natural outgrowth of his opinion in *Right to Choose v. Byrne*. Writing for the majority, Justice Pollock explained that New Jersey would depart from the federal precedent that pregnant women do not have the right to public funding for abortions to protect their health. In finding that the New Jersey statute prohibiting public funding for such abortions was forbidden by the state Constitution, he wrote:

> Thus, the statute impinges upon the fundamental right of a woman to control her body and destiny. That right encompasses one of the most intimate decisions in human experience, the choice to terminate a pregnancy or bear a child. This intensely personal decision is one that should be made by a woman in consultation with trusted advisers, such as her doctor, but without undue government interference. In this case, however, the State admittedly seeks to influence the decision between abortion and childbirth. Indeed, it concedes that, for a woman who cannot afford either medical procedure, the statute skews the decision in favor of childbirth at the expense of the mother's health.

Justice Pollock had an equal respect for national sovereignty. His dissent in *Hunter v. Greenwood Trust Company* was vindicated when the U.S. Supreme Court reversed the majority's holding that federal law did not pre-empt state regulation of credit-card lending practices.

As a result of his interest in personal rights guaranteed under state constitutions, Justice Pollock developed a national expertise in the intersection of law and medicine. His 1989 Vanderbilt Lecture, republished in 41 Rutgers L. Rev. 505, has been cited in all the leading American articles on the subject. His opinion in *Procanik v. Cillo* delicately balanced legal and moral choices. In that case, the Court allowed an infant to recover extraordinary medical expenses for injuries caused by a negligent diagnosis during prenatal care even if the parents' claims were time-barred. He reasoned that "[l]aw is more than an exercise in logic, and logical analysis, although essential to a system of ordered justice, should not become an instrument of injustice."

His good friend, former Maine Chief Justice Daniel Wathen, liked to kid him about his role in the Court's life-and-death decisions. "You have a 1,000 percent better chance of dying in a nursing home in New Jersey than if you get the death penalty," Wathen said.

Like Justice Handler, Justice Pollock was not an abstract theorist. He wrote hundreds of common-law decisions for the Court, each marked by sparing prose and clarity of expression. Memorable to me was *Buckley v. Trenton Saving Fund Society*, in which Justice Pollock delineated the limits of a cause of action for intentional infliction of emotional distress involving negligent commercial acts. In weighing the rights of banks and their customers, Justice Pollock wrote:

In striking that balance, we recognize that banks often conduct their business through branches, and that customers often do business with more than one branch of the same bank. The result is that over-the-counter transactions are often impersonal, a situation that can create tension between the customer's interest in cashing checks and the bank's interest in verifying the identity of its customers. In this setting, the system sometimes malfunctions. To some extent, slight emotional distress arising from the occasional dishonor of a check is one of the regrettable aggravations of living in today's society.

In the everyday work of the Court, he was a gifted member of the ensemble. He was the Lewis F. Powell Jr. of the New Jersey Supreme Court, a justice of impeccable scholarship and courtly manner. His questioning at oral arguments was always conversational, never confrontational. In conference, he was never didactic, never doctrinaire.

During his early years on the bench, Justice Pollock chaired the Court's Judiciary Information Systems Policy Committee. He shepherded the New Jersey courts into the information age in the use of computers and electronic services. As one of the first members of the Court to use a personal computer, he developed the practice of composing his opinions on a word processor. I believe that this led to his sparse but beautiful prose style. I am certain that the average length of his opinions was much shorter than that of the other members of the Court and his choice of words more selective.

Although terse, Justice Pollock's opinions were eloquent. In his widely quoted article, "The Art of Judging,"

71 N.Y.U. L. Rev. 591 (1996), he explained that a legal opinion should be like a work of art that must be perceived as beautiful in itself:

> Great judicial opinions resemble "high art," and some are of museum quality. At times, however, the judicial process, like artistic creation, may lack the glamour of the end result. Michelangelo, lying on a scaffold, neck aching, with paint dripping on his face, must have had doubts about the glory of painting the ceiling in the Sistine Chapel. Likewise, even the most dedicated judges, working in isolation, confronted with an unending procession of cases and worried about their daily preparation, may wonder about the nobility of their calling.

> Like judges, artists make critical factual judgments. They ask: What shall I include? What shall I emphasize? How shall I depict my subject? Another similarity is that both judges and artists work within constraints. An artist cannot make a canvas larger than it is. Nor can the artist convert canvas into another medium.

Justice Pollock encountered these constraints in composing one of his early opinions, *O'Keeffe v. Snyder*. That case dealt with the right of artist Georgia O'Keeffe to recover her lost paintings despite a statute-of-limitations claim. He discussed ordinary legal doctrine with characteristic richness. "Properly interpreted," he wrote, "the discovery rule becomes a vehicle for transporting equitable considerations into the statute of limitations for replevin." His use of allusion and metaphor to paint the setting of life and law was especially effective. One of his most notable passages was contained in *Schroeder v. Perkel*, in which he wrote: "A family is woven of the fibers of life; if one strand is damaged, the whole structure may suffer. The filaments of family life, although individually spun, create a web of interconnected legal interests."

In the field of criminal law, he was unflinching in enforcement of the Fourth Amendment. Of all the members of the Court, he possessed the greatest sense of respect for the privacy of individuals. In his dissent in *State v. Bruzzese*, he concluded that "the invalidation of [a] pretextual search would not impair efficient law enforcement, but it would preserve a paramount constitutional right."

Stewart Pollock had been in private practice and had served as an assistant U.S. attorney, a Board of Public Utilities commissioner, a State Commission of Investigation member and chief counsel to Brendan Byrne, left, when the governor nominated him to the state Supreme Court in 1979.

His death-penalty jurisprudence displayed a strong commitment to the role of the jury as the essential connection between capital punishment and the civilized norms of society. In *State v. Bey* II, he wrote:

In capital cases, jury sentencing constitutes a link between contemporary community values and the penal system. Without that link, the determination of punishment could hardly reflect "the evolving standards of decency that mark the progress of a maturing society." ... When the jury speaks, it is as the conscience of the community. As important as correct jury instructions are to all criminal cases, they are even more crucial in a capital case because of the jury's responsibility to decide whether a defendant shall live or die.

Justice Pollock was at home in every setting. He was a national leader in the field of products liability law. The law was shaped by his opinions in *O'Brien v. Muskin Corporation* (state-of-the-art evidence is admissible in strict liability cases pertaining to defectively designed products); *Alloway v. General Marine Industries L.P.* (U.C.C. express warranty provisions provide the exclusive remedy for economic loss incurred as a result of damage to luxury boat); *Baird v. American Medical Optics* (statute of limitations begins to run when the plaintiff is aware, or reasonably should be aware, of facts indicating that she or he has been injured through the fault of another); and *Mettinger v. Globe Slicing Machine Co. Inc.* (product-line exception to indemnify successor manufacturers is permitted).

In *Pierce v. Ortho Pharmaceutical Corporation*, he re-defined the employment-at-will doctrine when he permit-ted the use of public-policy exceptions in cases of wrongful termination. In *Sica v. Board of Adjustment of Township of Wall*, he clarified what constitutes an inherently ben-eficial zoning use. In *Herman v. Sunshine Chemical Specialties, Inc.*, he delineated the standards for awards of punitive damages.

Justice Pollock liked to kid me about my judicial icons. Once, discussing a habeas corpus case, he composed a pyr-amid of my values. "Attorney X" in the box shown here is a redacted reference to an attorney who appeared before us wearing Gucci loafers without socks and sipping a Coke. It did not make a good impression on the Court.

Justice Pollock and his wife, Penny, had many diverse interests beyond the law. In the 1990s, he and Penny de-cided that it was time to tango, and they dutifully em-barked on a course of tango lessons. We could always tell when he had a tango lesson. He would start twitching if the conference threatened to drag on so long as to in-terfere with a lesson. I do not think we caused him to miss even one. He and Penny loved to travel and learn new things. In 1991, they planned a trip to France. Chief Justice Wilentz, hearing of their plans, sent them, as he did to each of us when we planned a trip, a long, single-spaced letter:

Dear Penny and Stu:

Accompanying this letter (I hope) are some materi-als concerning

Provence, the Riviera, and Paris. I am afraid they do not help you in your major goal, finding a place to stay where Penny can become Mrs. Matisse.

While Jackie and I saw a lot of Provence and the Riviera, we invariably stayed at expensive hotels and you do not need any special perception or guidance to find out which ones they are. Where to go to paint, I do not know. Jackie always brought her little note pad with her on which she made drawings, but she usually made them from the hotel room or from wherever we happened to be. There are things to see and to paint all over the area, as I guess there are everywhere, and in particular outstanding views of the sea, the cliffs overlooking the sea, the people overlooking the cliffs and the sea, and just about everything else along the Riviera, extending, at least as far as I am concerned, from Monte Carlo all along the coast to Saint Tropez. Technically, it may go farther. Going inland from there, still probably within the Riviera, although perhaps bordering on Provence, there is Vence and San Paul de Vence and Cagnes, all a very short distance from Nice, all up in the mountains, all absolutely beautiful both within the towns and in the approaches to the towns. There are hills, valleys, roads, lanes, churches, museums, streams, all you need is a little ink and white paper.

If you move inland from Cannes, you will run across Grasse, way up high, and on your way there you will

see some absolutely splendid sights, quite suitable
for painting if you have nothing better to do. There
are two lovely peninsulas along the Riviera, one is
Saint-Jean-Cap-Ferrat, the other Cap d'Antibes.
Cap d'Antibes is worth traveling even if you do not
paint just to see the incredible homes on the peninsula and also the Eden Roc Hotel if you want to
see the way the not so beautiful people live. Saint
Jean Cap Ferrat is very close to where Jackie and I
regularly stayed, at La Reserve Hotel in Beaulieu?
It is a nice place to have a drink. But the Voile d'Or
on Saint Jean Cap Ferrat is also a nice place to
have a drink and you can stay there, maybe. It is
a beautiful little peninsula. The whole Riviera in
the middle of summer is wildly touristy, but really
worth seeing. If you are in Provence and you get
some time you really ought to take a look at it. And
Monte Carlo is definitely worth seeing. Just to see
it. The casino is not worth it.

● ● ●

Whatever else you do, remember you are on a vacation. And remember most of all that you will return
again, and again, and again and that what you
should do is enjoy yourself, see what you happen
to want to, what you happen to run into, but never
for one second have the slightest anxiety about not
seeing enough. Do you like to get up at 11:00 in the
morning? Then get up at 11:00. Do you like to walk
around aimlessly — do so. Do you like to read about

a church 30 miles away but not go to see it — then don't see it. You'll see it next time. Maybe you will never see it. Maybe it will burn down. Enjoy the day. It is almost impossible not to enjoy yourself on this kind of a vacation unless you make one big mistake, and that is trying to do too much, trying to see too much, feeling the pressure of a schedule, a plan, a list of things that you simply must do or see. Next year will be soon enough, the year after or the year after. Enjoy your vacation *this* year. For instance, a typical day: you wake up, wherever you are, find a little place where you can get a nice little continental breakfast, consisting solely of croissants, as only the French can make them, and cafe filch, their marvelous coffee. There will be butter and jam and you will have had enough. If you must have orange juice have it, but you will pay through the nose. Bring vitamins.

Then just walk around, anywhere, just a little walk. I assume at some point you will rent a car so just drive around. Keep your eye open for a place that looks as if it might be nice for lunch, or if you are in the mood, buy some of your own things and have lunch wherever you happen to be living. That can get a little bit like work, or fun, depending upon your mood. If you want to, take a look at the Michelin or a Pat Wells book and see if there are any places in the area that would be nice for lunch. In the Riviera and I guess in all of Provence there is something called pan bagna (probably spelled a million different ways) it is a roll or a piece of bread with oil, vinegar, tuna, and I forget what else. It is great. Or a sandwich mixture consisting of a baget, their marvelous bread, with butter, jambon (ham), and fromage (cheese). Add some nice hot mustard, request un pichet de vin rouge (a little pitcher of red wine) and you are in heaven. Not only that, you have had a very light lunch and you are ready for a big dinner if you are in the mood.

Do not eat two important meals during the day, only one. Unless you cannot resist. Having decided where you will have lunch, go back to your room, bring a newspaper, and relax. Maybe that afternoon after lunch you will hop in the car, drive about six miles to another place, walk around there for an hour or so, and then return. Go to sleep. Turn on the TV, maybe they have CNN. Get the International Herald Tribune, find out what is going on in the world. Pick out a place for dinner. And on, and on, and on. *Don't* get up at 6:00 in the morning, slug down your breakfast, hop in the car and go to 15 towns, 12 museums, 4 art galleries, choking your lunch in, off to a mountain, finally, back home, exhausted, incredibly tired, unhappy, etc.

Enough advice. You'll discover your own pace soon enough.

Do not forget to have bouillabaisse or, if you are not in the mood for big chunks of the seafood right in the soup, then something that is a little bit less world class, but something that a lot of people like a lot more, and that is bourride or soup poison, both of them probably meaning fish soup, essentially tasting a great deal like bouillabaisse, but without any fish swimming around in it, topped with something called rouille which is a marvelous gelatinous thing that is essentially garlic. You eat that with a piece of bread and butter and you are in heaven. I don't mean to knock bouillabaisse, it is marvelous too. It is a whole meal. It's got lobsters, crabs, other kinds of fish in it. And, of course, when you are on the Riviera fish is a great thing since it is fresh. There is a little village called Eze, there may be two of them, one of them is way, way, way up high in the mountains, and it has a couple of hotels one is called Chateau d'Eze and a marvelous view where, if the day is clear, you can see an awful long distance and a lot of beautiful things. A rather expensive restaurant, however. Always find out what the restaurant costs before you set foot in it. And all of the French restaurants have their prices posted outside.

Lest this become a book I'll stop.
Sincerely,

In addition to his interest in travel, Justice Pollock is known for his thriftiness. I recall him saying that once, when attending an American Law Institute conference in Philadelphia, he gave a ride in his Honda with 115,000 miles on it to Geoffrey C. Hazard Jr., a national expert on legal ethics. That prompted Hazard to ask, "Do you drive this to prove your integrity?" And when the justice retired, *The Star-Ledger* of Newark wrote on Feb. 26, 1999, "Wearing the same suit he wore 20 years ago when he was appointed to the high Court — a testament to his frugality and fitness — Pollock reported to work at his Morristown office as usual yesterday and sent his letter of resignation to [Gov. Christine Todd] Whitman early in the morning."

PHOTO COURTESY OF DANIEL J. O'HERN

Stewart Pollock, shown here with his wife, Penny, delicately balanced legal and moral choices in *Procanik v. Cillo*. The Court allowed an infant to recover extraordinary medical expenses for injuries caused by a negligent diagnosis during prenatal care, even if the parents' claims were time-barred.

Lastly, I must speak of Justice Pollock's visceral distaste for people who did not respect the truth. He cannot stand people who lie. In *Massachusetts Mutual Life Insurance Company v. Manzo*, he deplored the conduct of a policyholder who misrepresented his medical history on an application. On Aug. 22, 1983, Manzo was found in the trunk of his car, shot to death. Notwithstanding this information, Massachusetts Mutual issued Manzo's policy on Aug. 31, 1983, effective June 13, 1983, at standard rates, with an annual premium of $1,345. After Manzo's death, the insurer conducted an investigation, which showed Manzo's undisclosed history of diabetes and related problems. Based on this information, Massachusetts Mutual sued to rescind the policy. Justice Pollock was not sympathetic to the family of the unfortunate victim. He wrote:

An insurer is entitled to relief when it relies on incorrect information provided by an insured in an insurance application if the information was material either to the insurer's decision to insure or to the terms of the contract. As the Legislature perceived ... the law should encourage insureds to tell the truth, not to conceal information from the insurer ...

And in *Kernan v. One Washington Park Urban Renewal Associates*, he condemned an attorney versed in half-truths:

More egregious examples of discovery abuse may exist. The nondisclosure in this case, however, suffices to make the point. Shenanigans have no place in a lawsuit. Modern litigation is too time consuming and expensive for courts to tolerate discovery abuses. For over fifty years, courts have endeavored to transform civil litigation from a battle royal to a search for truth.

I first met Justice Pollock in 1978 when we both joined Gov. Byrne's administration. He was more than a colleague for more than 20 years. Like him, I went from the governor's office to the New Jersey Supreme Court. I often sought his counsel. I missed him greatly when he retired in 1999, a year before I did.

6
Doc

We called Justice Garibaldi "Doc" because she collected so many honorary degrees. Almost every May, at least one institution of higher education would confer on her an honorary doctorate. She deserved them all.

Justice Garibaldi was the first woman to serve on the Supreme Court or its predecessors. Gov. Thomas H. Kean announced her appointment on Sept. 28, 1982, and Justice Garibaldi was sworn in on Nov. 17 of that year.

A specialist in tax law, she was a partner at what is now Riker, Danzig, Scherer, Hyland and Perretti in Morristown. Before joining that firm, she was on the staff of the Internal Revenue Service's New York regional counsel. (Of course, whenever we had a tax case, Justice Garibaldi would say: "I *didn't* do that kind of tax work.")

At the time of her nomination, she was president of the New Jersey State Bar Association. She also was a trustee of St. Peter's College as well as a director of the New Jersey Chamber of Commerce, New Jersey Bell Telephone Co. and Washington Savings Bank.

Justice Garibaldi was born in Jersey City on Nov. 26, 1934. She graduated from Connecticut College in 1956 and Columbia University School of Law in 1959, was admitted to the bar the next year and received her master's degree in tax law from New York University in 1963.

Justice Garibaldi's life was one of firsts. We used to say, "she does not want to belong to any organization unless she is the only woman in it." She was the first woman to serve as president of the State Bar Association and as a member of the Essex Club in Newark, a stately English Georgian Revival structure built in 1926 as a place where business leaders could mingle.

Justice Clifford remembered her this way in a tribute published in the spring of 2000 in the Rutgers Law Journal:

She will live to be 118. Optimistic, cheerful, busy, involved, outwardly-focused, resourceful, smart (in many ways, including "street" smart), she always seems to have things pretty well under control — because she does. You're going to have to get up very early in the morning if you're going to beat Marie Garibaldi. (In fact, in the twelve years that we served together I think I arrived at the Justice Complex or the Chief's chambers before she did exactly once, and that was because she had had a flat.)

When Justice Garibaldi arrived at the Court in 1982 — the first woman ever appointed to that position (are we *still* making a big point of that?) — various institutions of higher learning fell all over themselves to award her honorary doctorate degrees. So help me, there must have been half a dozen of them in the first two years, as a consequence of which she picked up the name "Doc."

PHOTO BY BILL KOSTROUN

In her trilogy of right-to-die cases, Marie Garibaldi emphasized the principles that pervade her jurisprudence: self-responsibility and self-determination.

Two things stand out in my recollection of Marie Garibaldi's time on the Court. The first is her unfailingly pleasant demeanor. With her, it was perfectly natural, not assumed. She could be forceful, even aggressive, in the discussion of cases; but if ever she felt exasperation or impatience (as I fear some of the rest of us did), she never revealed it.

The second is her eminent good sense and sound judgment. How many times did she snap us back to reality with a pithy observation such as "You people are nuts!" when we were blathering away on an intellectual frolic and detour? Her feet were on the ground, always, and thank goodness she was there to make sure that the rest of us didn't take flight.

Justice Garibaldi was enormously productive during her 18 years on the Court. She authored more than 230 opinions, many of them of major significance. From her first day on the Court, she displayed the openness that was characteristic of her entire service. Her opinions were direct and comprehensive. Chief Justice Wilentz entrusted to her the most sensitive of our decisions because he sensed that there would be universal respect and that no hidden agenda lay behind the decision.

We liked to joke about the fact that she was naturally photogenic and a darling of the press. She was such a favorite of the media that on one occasion, a local newspaper printed her photograph with a story announcing the reappointment of Justice Stein to a tenured term. One of the Court's clerks was moved to write the following parody:

The Statewide Gazette, Friday, December 20, 1991

Garibaldi Colleague Wins Reappointment to Supreme Court; Senators Unanimously Approve Justice Until Retirement

The New Jersey Senate yesterday gave tenure on the Supreme Court to a colleague of Justice Marie Garibaldi, the only woman ever to serve on the State's highest court. "I'm delighted for old What's-his-Face," said Madam Justice, "but am concerned that now that he's secure in the job, he'll become a major pain in the prat rather than just a stubborn mule," she added, with an airy wave in the general direction of Bergen County.

Justice Garibaldi's newly tenured colleague tried to offer a word or two, but nobody paid him any heed. The press's attention was fixed on the Court's youngest member, who, however, appeared to be preoccupied with her intensive study of the Bluebook and travel brochures. Oh — the name of her tenured colleague is Stein — first name Gary, as in "Gari-baldi."

Justice Garibaldi's signature opinions were in the trilogy of right-to-die cases, *In re Farrell, In re Peter* and *In re Jobes*, in which she emphasized the principles that pervade her jurisprudence: self-responsibility and self-determination.

Justice Garibaldi was the architect of our gender-discrimination law, most notably with her decision in *Lehmann v. Toys 'R'Us, Inc.* The Chief Justice entrusted her with matters of delicate constitutional balance, as in the case of *Communications Workers of America v. Florio*, in which she upheld the constitutional principle of separation of powers that permitted the governor to exercise the authority to implement layoffs. No one ever questioned her independence.

She was a protector of free speech, as in *Costello v. Ocean County Observer, Turf Lawnmower Repair, Inc. v. Bergen Record Corporation* and *Ward v. Zelikovsky*. She was especially gifted in the areas of her expertise, such as corporate affairs and taxation. Her opinions in *Brenner v. Berkowitz* and *Lawson Mardon Wheaton, Inc. v. Smith* defined the internal management of corporations. In *Sons of Thunder, Inc. v. Borden, Inc.*, she dealt with fairness in contract negotiations.

PHOTO COURTESY OF DANIEL J. O'HERN

Marie Garibaldi displayed an openness that led Robert Wilentz to give her the most sensitive cases because he sensed her decisions would engender universal respect. Shown from left, during the Association of the Federal Bar of New Jersey ceremony in 1994 honoring U.S. Supreme Court Justice David Souter, are Garibaldi, Gary Stein, Daniel O'Hern, Morris Pashman and Souter.

We sometimes called Justice Garibaldi the "Iron Lady." And for anyone who doubts she was tough, *State v. Priester* is an example of why she got the name. In that case, a convicted rapist sought to be released from his prison sentence on the basis of a medical disability. He had incurred his unfortunate injuries in a fall from the second story of the Bergen County Jail while trying to escape. He managed to land astride a fence, suffering diminished use of his legs and impairment of bladder, bowel and sexual functions. You can imagine what happened. After a sympathetic analysis of the record and medical testimony, Justice Garibaldi was constrained to conclude that the evidence did not demonstrate that the defendant's condition had so deteriorated from the date of the sentence as to warrant clemency. She added for emphasis: "We also find it relevant that defendant's serious injury and resultant illness were the direct result of his own criminal behavior."

Justice Garibaldi, however, was not a clone of Margaret Thatcher, the model of an Iron Lady at the time. In *Baumann v. Marinaro*, she recognized the need for flexibility in the law to see that justice was done when service of process had been improperly made on an individual. In *Lowe v. Zarghami*, she upheld the right of patients to sue when they were not aware that their physicians were public employees entitled to certain immunities.

Justice Garibaldi wrote many important capital punishment decisions, including *State v. Martini*, *State v. DiFrisco* and *State v. Muhammad*, involving victim-impact statements. In the area of criminal procedure, she insisted on fairness in the administration of the criminal justice system through uniform procedural guidelines for extended sentencing. She was the master of complexity, too, as in *Waterson v. General Motors Corporation*, a difficult case involving enhanced damages for injuries caused by the failure to use a seat belt. And in *Cesare v. Cesare*, she defined the parental rights of visitation and custody.

Equally important to the life of the Court were Justice Garibaldi's dissenting opinions. In *State v. Novembrino*, she departed from the Court's view that the New Jersey Constitution did not embrace a good-faith exception to the exclusionary rule. Her views on constitutional freedom of expression are expansive. The so-called liberal wing of the Court was too willing, in her view, to curtail speech it did not like. She joined the dissent in *In the Matter of the Petition of Felmeister & Isaacs* and would have restrained the Court's regulation of attorney advertising. And in *In the Matter of Norma Randolph*, she would have similarly loosened the Court's rein on the free-speech rights of judicial employees.

Justice Garibaldi and I agreed in several dissents — notably in *Devlin v. Mayor and Council, City of Ocean City*, where we would not have reinstated Sunday closing laws that we believed were pre-empted by the Code of Criminal Justice. In *Fischer v. Johns-Manville Corporation*, we argued for more stringent standards in the imposition of punitive damages. And in *Christian Science Board of Directors of the First Church of Christ, Scientist v. Evans*, we found that there was adequate, substantial and credible evidence to support the trial court's holding that "Christian Science Church" is a protectable trademark because it is a descriptive term that signifies a church's affiliation with the mother church. Our most unfortunately worded dissent was in *State v. Serrone*, in which we believed that the Code of Criminal Justice, as originally enacted, did not contemplate consecutive life sentences for two murders. The press reported that "O'Hern and Garibaldi side with the murderer."

Justice Garibaldi's most famous dissent is, of course, *Kelly v. Gwinnell*. Justice Clifford circulated to us a collection of essays published less than three weeks later, on July 14, 1984, in the London *Spectator* in which British humorist Auberon Waugh satirized the sanctimonious attitude of temperance fanatics. Waugh wrote:

> To measure the extremes to which these anti-drink fanatics are prepared to go, one must look across at the other side of the herring pond where the New Jersey Supreme Court ruled by a six to one majority last month that a host who gave his guests liquor was liable (no less than a publican) for injury to other parties caused by the guests' subsequent drunk driving. As the one dissenting voice from this absurd ruling (Judge Marie Garibaldi, God bless her) pointed out, it means that hosts will in the future have to monitor their guests' drinking.

Well, of course, that's not something Justice Garibaldi would want anyone to do.

Similarly important to the work of the Court were her contributions to the field of alternative dispute resolution. Chief Justice Wilentz appointed her chair of the committee that developed the most comprehensive system of arbitration, mediation and dispute resolution in the nation.

Finally, she was the most agreeable of colleagues, as was made evident in a series of light-hearted poems various justices wrote on the occasion of her fifth anniversary on the Court. Here is one written by Justice Stein and his wife, Et:

PHOTO BY DANIEL J. O'HERN

Shown from left, Barbara O'Hern, Marie Garibaldi and the justice's mother, Marie Garibaldi, at Newark International Airport on Oct. 4, 1995, to witness the arrival of Pope John Paul II.

ODE TO MARIE

On New Jersey's high Court of renown,
Six malcontents grimace and frown,
'Cause they work night and day for miserly pay,
While Marie's always out on the town.

Six scholars so steeped in the law,
Their opinions have scarcely a flaw
But ever since Marie said the host is home free,
She's the one that the bar holds in awe.

So tonight as you end your fifth year,
Surrounded by clerks and good cheer,
Remember your guys — dull, plodding but wise,
You're the only one who knows that we're here!
Love, Et and Gary

The many poems prompted this response from Justice
Garibaldi to her colleagues:

ODE TO MY BRETHREN

London, Paris, Moscow, or Rome
Some of you think I scarcely am home
And while my dear brethren prepare our next
    tome
It is said that the House of Savoy I do roam.

Though you may think my approach too
    precarious
And wonder how I could be so darn gregarious
I know all too well that your thrill is vicarious
And you chalk it all up to "Marie the hilarious."

Oh! Brethren of mine allow me to say
All work and no play your hairs will make grey
Make time for some bubbly and terrine de pâté
You'll find it brings laughter and joy to your day.

All kidding aside, all jest put to rest
I venture to say that you guys are the best
And though you may think me a fun loving pest
I know to replace you would be a futile quest.
With my sincere thanks for your many kindnesses
    to me through the years. MLG

In tribute to her good companionship, Justice Handler named one of his newborn Williamsburg-bred sheep Marie, and we closely followed her progress. And when news of sheep cloning made international headlines, one of the justices created this magazine cover:

ILLUSTRATION COURTESY OF DANIEL J. O'HERN

Alan Handler named one of his sheep after Marie Garibaldi in recognition of her agreeable nature, prompting one of the Court members to create a mock magazine cover when sheep-cloning made the news.

7
Wall Street

That is what we called Justice Stein. He was the only member of our Court who had been a Wall Street lawyer. He took pride in that fact and offered us constant reminders of how they did things there.

We had an empty feeling when Justice Stein announced his intention to retire in September 2002 after 17 years of service. He was the last member of the group of justices on the Wilentz Court who had served together for a decade. His retirement marked the end of that era, but reminded us of the continuity of the Court.

Justice Stein was born in Newark on June 13, 1933. He lived much of his youth in Irvington and liked to describe for us his old neighborhood. He earned a scholarship to Duke University, graduating from its college in 1954 and its law school in 1956, second in his class. He was an associate editor of the Duke Law Journal but found time to referee Duke basketball scrimmages. According to Justice Stein, he could play almost as well as Dick Groat, an All-American basketball player in the early 1950s.

After graduation from law school, Justice Stein specialized in corporate and antitrust law with the New York firm of Kramer, Marx, Greenlee & Backus until 1966, when he established a solo practice in Paramus. From 1972 to 1982, he was a partner in the Paramus firm of Stein and Kurland.

During his Wall Street years, he was called up to active duty at the time of the Berlin Wall crisis in 1961. While on recall, he met another young reservist, Thomas Kean. Little did he know that his soldier buddy would become governor, invite him into his cabinet and announce his intention on Nov. 7, 1984, to appoint him to the New Jersey Supreme Court. He was serving as director of Gov. Kean's Office of Policy and Planning at the time.

Justice Stein was the first of our members to insist that he needed a third clerk. This led to endless attacks on his work habits, and we were regularly treated to Justice Clifford's cartoons depicting Justice Stein's chambers.

Justice Stein's Wall Street mentality produced an extraordinary blend of dogged preparation, attention to detail and relentless determination to unravel any case. No case was too small for his attention; no case was too big for his intellect.

We best saw the results of his preparation in that series of decisions involving public funding of education known as the *Abbott v. Burke* cases. In this, as in so many areas of the law, his tireless preparation paid off by revealing at oral argument the strength or weakness in a case. I remember so clearly the oral argument in *Abbott v. Burke* IV. That case concerned the constitutionality of the Comprehensive Educational Improvement and Financing Act of 1996 (CEIFA), Gov. Whitman's effort to remedy constitutional violations resulting from disparities in the state's system of elementary and secondary public school funding. Education advocates feared that without the leadership of Chief Justice Wilentz, who died in 1996, the Court would retreat from its mandates.

PHOTO BY CARMEN NATALE

The *Abbott* school funding cases were illustrative of Gary Stein's approach: relentless groundwork that revealed a case's strength or weakness at argument.

The case was heard on March 3, 1997. Peter Verniero, New Jersey's attorney general, argued on behalf of the state. Justice Stein knew as much about the intricate provisions of the new law as did the law's sponsors. What follows is a partial transcript of that oral argument concerning a funding model for the state's special-needs districts. CEIFA's funding model provided $6,700 per inner-city pupil, compared with the $11,000 per pupil provided under Gov. James Florio's Quality Education Act of 1990 (QEA):

> JUSTICE STEIN: General Verniero, that's a comforting response to know that the model can be adjusted but the reason I ask about the model, and I am glad you focused on it early, is because this new law, as we know, allows richer suburban districts to spend more money than the special-needs districts; and so in deciding whether this new law is going to assure a thorough and efficient education, the cost assumptions that the State has made are so critical. And I want to acknowledge the [Core Curriculum] standards. The standards are very impressive. In fact, they are somewhat intimidating to me because when I read some of those standards and found that the requirements for fourth graders were more challenging than I would care to assume, I recognize the standards are very telling; but we have a record in the case, and the record was made, as you know, in the late eighties before Administrative Law Judge [Steven] Lefelt and the record reflected the abysmal conditions that existed in some of our urban schools at that time and the tremendous difference between what the urban schools were achieving and what the suburban schools were achieving, the tremendous disparity in facilities, the paucity of special science equipment and laboratories, the absence of

foreign languages, the absence of adequate teachers. Now, we haven't updated the record, but we know from what we read in the newspaper that on the high school proficiency tests scores published in December the State average was 75.6%. Some of the urban districts are continuing to perform at a very low level — East Orange 30.2%, Trenton 20.6% passing, Henry Snyder School in Jersey City, a takeover district, 16.8%, Barringer High School in Newark 11.7%, East Side High School in Paterson 17.4% passing, compared to the State average. So, I looked at the model and had the concern about whether the model fairly reflected the cost to a typical urban district of preparing those children to learn to these very ambitious standards and what I saw in the model, as you just confirmed, was that the model has nothing to do, from the standpoint of its calculations, with the devastating conditions in some of our urban districts. It doesn't purport to recognize that in Trenton the need for security guards is far more than what the model says or that in Paterson and Jersey City the need for new facilities and better bathrooms and science equipment is way below what the suburban schools possess, so I wonder how we can have confidence in a model that [is] based on a typical district but that doesn't concern itself with poor urban districts. How can we have confidence that the $6,700 figure for elementary school districts in the model is going to equip the urban school students to learn these very difficult standards.

ATTORNEY GENERAL: I think there are several responses, Justice Stein. First and perhaps foremost in a strict legal sense, we have to presume the experts who make these judgments make sound decisions ... which is why, of course, these agency actions [are accorded deference].

JUSTICE STEIN: Well, deference would be very tempting, but on the face of it, it looks like they used as their base statistics information that has nothing to do with what's going on in Newark and Jersey City and Trenton and Camden.

The Supreme Court essentially adopted the theory of the case set forth in the exchange between Justice Stein and Attorney General Verniero. The Court required that funding for special-needs districts take account of "what's going on in Newark and Jersey City and Trenton and Camden." The Court held, in an opinion by Justice Handler, that although CEIFA's standards defining the substantive content of "education" to be provided to public school students were facially adequate and consistent with the Constitution's Thorough and Efficient Education Clause, CEIFA's funding standards were unconstitutional as applied to special-needs districts and CEIFA's funding levels were insufficient to permit those districts to provide a thorough and efficient education to inner-city children. In addition, the Court held that CEIFA's failure to address the problem of dilapidated, unsafe and overcrowded facilities in the special-needs districts violated the education clause.

In *Abbott* VI, Justice Stein wrote in a separate concurring opinion of the vision that had driven him:

The longstanding inability of urban public schools throughout the nation to provide an adequate education to minority students from low-income families represents the most enduring public policy failure of my generation. For much of the past fifty years state governments generally were unwilling to focus on the ills of urban schools. Over the past two decades, however, the issue has attracted both state and national attention. Throughout the country reforms in urban education have been implemented and found wanting. In major cities, new superintendents are hired and fired with regularity. Candidates for public office promise to repair urban education, but the promises are seldom kept and, when implemented, rarely succeed.

In New Jersey, as in other states, failures in urban education have led education advocates to turn to our courts for relief. For the twenty-five years following this Court's first disposition in school funding litigation, see *Robinson v. Cahill*, 62 N.J. 473 (1973), the focus has been on fiscal parity. Recently, the emphasis has shifted from funding equity to educational adequacy.

Justice Stein was a perfectionist. He expected of others what he gave himself. He could not abide what he considered bureaucratic inefficiencies in the implementation of court-ordered mandates for urban schools. He deplored the use by the commissioner of education of a "form letter" that categorically rejected the requests of school districts to meet the special needs of students, an approach he viewed as "formalistic and inflexible" and inconsistent with the Court's expectations. He wrote in the concurrence in *Abbott* VI:

> Only two years have elapsed since *Abbott* V was decided. As evidenced by the Court's disposition of this Motion, significant adjustments in approach and in implementation of the *Abbott* V reforms periodically may be required in the interest of the children whose education and future prospects are at stake. In an undertaking of this complexity, missteps are virtually certain to occur. However, those missteps and the resulting course corrections will be long forgotten if, over time, the reform efforts now under way succeed. But the clock is ticking, and for each school year in which implementation is delayed or flawed, thousands of urban children will lose the full benefit promised by the *Abbott* initiatives. The time for bold, corrective and decisive action by the DOE is now.

The final chapter came in 2002 in *Abbott* VIII. Justice Stein wrote in his dissent:

> This proceeding marks the fifteenth occasion in less than thirty years that the advocates of equal educational opportunity for poor urban school

children have come to this Court to seek judicial relief from inadequate funding, deficient substantive educational programs and substandard facilities. A concise summary of the history of the *Robinson v. Cahill* and *Abbott v. Burke* school litigation through 1998 is set forth in *Abbott v. Burke*, 153 N.J. 480, 490-93, 710 A.2d 450 (1998) (*Abbott V*). That summary reveals that in the course of this thirty-year-old litigation four state statutes providing for state funding of public education have been held by this Court to be unconstitutional as applied to the poorest urban school districts: The State School Incentive Equalization Aid Law (L.1970 c. 234); The Public School Education Act of 1975 (L.1975, c. 212); The Quality Education Act of 1990 (L.1990, c. 52); The Comprehensive Educational Improvement and Financing Act (CEIFA) (L.1996, c. 1389). Each one of those statutes, enacted by the Legislature and signed by the then Governor, was found to be flawed by this Court because of a failure to provide a level of funding "adequate to provide for the special educational needs of these poorer urban districts, and address their extreme disadvantages." *Abbott v. Burke*, 119 N.J. 287, 385, 575 A.2d 359 (1990) (*Abbott II*).

• • •

This Court has a unique role in this late stage of the approximately thirty-year history of urban school litigation in New Jersey. At every step of the long and arduous path leading to funding adequacy and essential substantive educational reforms, this Court has been required to act as the catalyst for urban school reform. Successful implementation of preschool in the *Abbott* districts, to a degree that will assure that the youngest children in those districts enter elementary school at grade level ready to learn, is among the most vital and indispensable components of that reform effort. Continued divisiveness among the community care providers, the districts, and the State can delay unduly the attainment of a successful preschool program for all eligible *Abbott* three-and four-year-olds. Confronted with the disarray revealed by this record, the Court's unwillingness to ensure implementation of its judgment mandating high quality preschool in the *Abbott* districts by the designation of a Special Master could be misunderstood to signal a lack of resolve and a dilution of the determination, perseverance, and consistency that has characterized the Court's educational reform decisions over the past three decades. By declining to appoint a Special Master to assist all parties in arriving at a uniform, efficient, responsible, and cohesive dispute resolution process, the Court risks perpetuating the high degree of frustration, antagonism, delay, and deficient implementation that have plagued the State's efforts these past four years. Unwilling to take that risk, I respectfully dissent from the Court's disposition.

PHOTO COURTESY OF DANIEL J. O'HERN

Gary Stein took crates of transcripts and briefs in the *State v. Marshall* post-conviction-relief case and worked all summer to reduce 500 claims of error to a manageable opinion. He is shown here on his bicycle next to Daniel O'Hern on Martha's Vineyard, where Stein invited the justices to prepare for the new term at his summer home.

Determination, perseverance and consistency. Those three words say a lot about Justice Stein. He is a bold and decisive man, but few bold and decisive people also have his tenacity. Sometimes those traits could become exasperating to the members of the Court. During one conference, for example, Justice Stein's unwillingness to revise an opinion prompted Justice Handler to say, "He writes with a scepter, not a pen."

But we always knew there was no hidden agenda

behind Justice Stein's drive, just the pursuit of justice as he saw it, in order to "get it right."

This determination was evident in every aspect of his work. Not a term of the Court passed that he did not labor for months to turn around the justices' thinking on a case or an issue. Sometimes he succeeded; sometimes he did not. In one ethics-disciplinary case, he unraveled the complexities of a real estate transaction and convinced the Court that what had at first glance appeared to be a plan to defraud was in fact a complex deal gone bad. Thus, a lawyer who was facing almost certain disbarment because of a disciplinary board's lack of understanding of the transaction was saved from that punishment.

His methods of persuasion took other forms as well. One example is *Troth v. State*, which concerned the duty of the state to maintain a dam. A boater had been drawn to his death at the unguarded dam's spillway. Justice Stein argued that a defective dam was a dangerous condition of property under the New Jersey Tort Claims Act. To reinforce his arguments, he urged Chief Justice Wilentz to read David McCullough's book, *The Johnstown Flood*, which recounts the loss of 2,209 lives.

Sometimes, he labored on lost causes. In *Kuzmicz v. Ivy Hill Park Apartments, Inc.*, he unsuccessfully tried to persuade the Court that a residential landlord owed a duty to warn a tenant of "off-premises" dangers that could be easily avoided by leaving the premises by another route.

And it was one of Justice Stein's memos that elicited a poignant response from the Chief Justice a month before he died, letting us know that he no longer had the strength to fight and that it was up to us to carry on:

June 25, 1996 Chief Justice Robert N. Wilentz
Supreme Court of New Jersey 257 Monmouth Road
Oakhurst, New Jersey 07755

Re: Brennan v. Orban A-95-96

Dear Chief Justice:

This case concerns the right to a jury trial for a
marital tort claim that is joined with a divorce action. At the conference, you, Jim [Justice James H.
Coleman Jr.] and I favored an expansive right to a
jury trial.

Dan's [Justice Daniel O'Hern's] opinion says all
the right things but on pages twenty-one and
twenty-two, when he gets to the bottom line, he
holds that the family part judge has the discretion
to try the case without a jury whenever the marital tort claim is "intertwined" with issues in the
divorce case. As a practical matter, I believe that
gives family part judges the freedom to allow very
few jury trials in marital tort cases. The dissent
goes sharply in the other direction. It may not be
as strong as your position at conference, but it categorically expresses a preference for jury trials in
almost every case.

I would welcome any suggestions. The question is
whether you want to participate in the opinion and
whether you want to join my dissent.

Sorry to bother you with this stuff but I know you had strong feelings about this case. Sincerely, Gary

PHOTO BY PHYLLIS E. TOWNSEND

Gary Stein was the last member of the Wilentz Court justices who had served together for a decade, and his retirement in 2002 marked the end of an era. Shown is the Court's retirement dinner for Stein and James Coleman Jr. on May 29, 2003, attended by sitting and past justices. From left are John Wallace Jr., Stewart Pollock, Jaynee LaVecchia, Court Clerk Stephen Townsend, Coleman, Virginia Long, Deborah Poritz, Peter Verniero, Alan Handler, Daniel O'Hern, Stein, Barry Albin, Marie Garibaldi, Robert Clifford, Sidney Schreiber and James Zazzali.

The Chief responded the same day, "I don't have the intellectual energy to make up my mind. Good luck! R.W."

There was no area of law that did not concern Justice

Stein. In *State v. Novembrino*, he recounted New Jersey's long experience with the exclusionary rule as a preface to our declining to follow *United States v. Leon* and *Massachusetts v. Sheppard* and to adopt the so-called good-faith exception to the requirement of obtaining a valid warrant. In *Carter-Wallace, Inc. v. Admiral Insurance Company*, he explained how excess insurance coverage for environmental damages should be allocated among successive policies. He was the Court's expert on zoning and planning matters. *Medici v. BPR Company* is a landmark opinion, reshaping the law for granting "special reasons variances." I liked to tell him that if he had made a better candidate (a not-so-obstinate one), he might have been elected mayor of Paramus, but would not have learned as much land-use law as he did as the attorney for the borough.

Justice Stein was a master of detail. When Chief Justice Wilentz assigned to him the opinion in the *State v. Marshall* post-conviction-relief case, Justice Stein took crates of transcripts and briefs to the porch of his home on Martha's Vineyard and worked all summer to reduce 500 claims of error to a manageable judicial opinion. Only a trace of dismay came through when he wrote: "An appeal based on so vast a record and implicating so many distinct issues obviously imposes an enormous institutional burden on this Court, diverting time and resources from the Court's other adjudicative and administrative responsibilities. We know that defendant faces the death penalty.

Nevertheless, we question both the wisdom and the necessity for so massive a presentation." Although I dissented from parts of his opinion, I respected the

breadth of its content. My son John, who was then a
deputy attorney general in the Appellate Section of the
state Division of Criminal Justice, said that almost every point of law that might need to be researched was in
that opinion.

Gary Stein spent a great deal of time trying to turn around his colleagues' thinking on a
case or issue. In one matter about the maintenance of a dam, he urged Robert Wilentz to
read *The Johnstown Flood*, which recounted the loss of 2,209 lives.

PHOTO BY THE STAR-LEDGER

Other memorable opinions include *Board of Education of Borough of Englewood Cliffs v. Board of Education of Borough of Tenafly* (holding that the state Board of Education has ultimate responsibility for developing and directing implementation of plan to redress racial imbalance at Dwight Morrow High School in Englewood); *Trantino v. New Jersey State Parole Board* (reversing the Parole Board's denial of parole because its determination that inmate was likely to recidivate was unsupported by preponderance of credible evidence); *In re Opinion 33 of the Committee on the Unauthorized Practice of Law* (applying public-interest standard and holding that neither engagement by New Jersey bond counsel of unlicensed lawyers in that firm or an out-of-state law firm to provide legal services through New Jersey bond counsel, nor direct retention of out-of-state law firm by New Jersey public issuer when required by special circumstances, will constitute the unauthorized practice of law); *Franklin Tower One, L.L.C. v. N.M.* (holding that state statute prohibiting landlords from refusing to rent to tenant because of "source of any lawful rent payment" bars landlords from refusing to accept federal Section 8 rental assistance voucher from an existing tenant); *Rendine v. Pantzer* (authorizing contingency enhancements in setting attorney-fee awards under New Jersey fee-shifting statutes); *Morton International, Inc. v. General Accident Insurance Company of America* (construing standard pollution-exclusion clause in manner consistent with objectively reasonable expectations of state regulatory authorities and holding that clause was enforceable only to extent of precluding coverage for insured's intentional discharge of known pollutants); and *In re Township of Warren* (holding invalid a Council on Affordable Housing regulation that authorized municipalities seeking substantive certification of fair-share plans for low-and moderate-cost housing to allocate 50 percent of such housing to income-eligible households whose occupants reside or work in the municipality).

In addition to determination and perseverance, Justice Stein had courage. He alone dissented from Chief Justice Wilentz's opinion in *Doe v. Poritz*. That opinion upheld the validity of Megan's Law, which requires notification to the community of the presence of convicted sex offenders. A tidal wave of public opinion favored the statute. In upholding the law, the Chief Justice wrote: "The essence of our decision is that the Constitution does not prevent society from attempting to protect itself from convicted sex offenders, no matter when convicted, so long as the means of protection are reasonably designed for that purpose and only for that purpose, and not designed to punish."

Justice Stein's response was:

Despite the Legislature's understandable concern about the danger presented by prior sex offenders, the judicial role, mindful of the compelling pressures that led to the statute's enactment, is to test the statute on the basis of the Constitution's fundamental protection against punitive retroactive legislation. I would hold that the devastating impact on prior sex offenders that will occur from implementation of [Megan's Law] constitutes retroactively imposed punishment prohibited by the Ex Post Facto Clause of the Constitution.

In *State v. Apprendi*, he dissented, with Justice Handler, from our decision to uphold the hate-crimes law that allowed a judge to impose an extended sentence of imprisonment if he or she found that the crime was motivated by racial bias. In an opinion I wrote, the Court concluded that the question of Apprendi's intent was a sentencing factor not requiring jury determination. In a 5-4 decision (I always remind Justice Stein of this), the U.S. Supreme Court accepted his viewpoint, declaring our law unconstitutional, because the statute allowed a judge, not a jury, to decide the sentence-enhancement factor. In *Apprendi v. New Jersey*, the Court held that the Sixth Amendment right to a jury trial, read in conjunction with the due-process requirement in the Fourteenth Amendment, requires that "any fact (other than prior conviction) that increases the maximum penalty for a crime must be charged in an indictment, submitted to a jury, and proven beyond a reasonable doubt." One justice of the U.S. Supreme Court made him right and me wrong. In the spring 2002 issue of *The Razor Wire*, a publication of The November Coalition, which advocates for drug-law reform, a prisoner wrote: "To the uninitiated, this [outcome] might seem like a 'no-brainer,' but the ramifications of the *Apprendi* case were the functional equivalent of logical shrapnel tearing through the nation's courts, both state and federal level."

Justice Stein's last opinion, *Lonegan v. State*, was a partial dissent from the Court's decision to defer judgment on the constitutionality of the issuance of so-called contract debt by independent state authorities without voter approval. In his view, the answer was clear: the issuance of any such debt that is backed solely by annual payments from the state budget, and not by independent revenues such as tolls, violates the Debt Limitation Clause of the New Jersey Constitution. He described as "a legal fiction" the state's argument that the Legislature has no obligation to appropriate the money to repay such bonds. He wrote: "The institutionally responsible answer is to recognize that the Constitution can be amended but it cannot be ignored." In his last opinion, he was still trying to get it right.

PHOTO BY STEPHEN W. TOWNSEND

Gary Stein, in center at podium, wrote a tribute for Robert Clifford's retirement dinner in December 1994 and sang it with Marie Garibaldi and Daniel O'Hern. Seated left to right are Clifford; his wife, Ruth; and Robert Wilentz. In the foreground is Sidney Schreiber, a former justice.

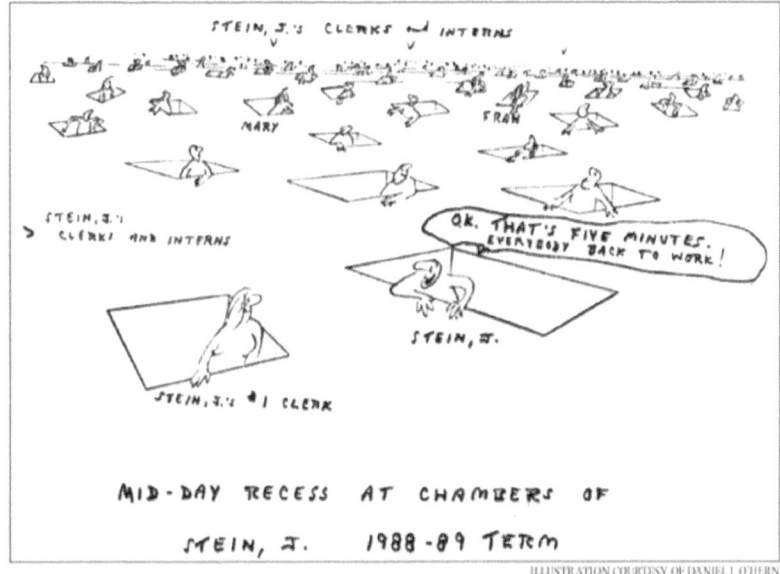

Robert Clifford took a cartoon he found and added his own commentary to reflect on Gary Stein's work habits.

Although occasionally vexing, Justice Stein was not a boring or one-dimensional colleague. He enjoyed theater and the arts, read widely and was a sports fan, although I accused him of being a front-runner. (He rooted for the football Giants, the Yankees and the Knicks.) I asked him whether he was rooting for the Nets in their late-season run for the championship in 2003. "Of course," he responded. He enjoyed frequent tennis games and regularly recalled for us accounts of his tennis partners' reactions to our decisions. He was a fitness fanatic. For some time, he baked oatmeal muffins for the Court that tasted every bit like baked oats, no more, no less. His law clerks became part of the Stein family that he loved so much. After every Thanksgiving recess, he would recall for us his exploits as quarterback during a Thanksgiving morning touch football game. Of course, he had to be quarterback. It was his ball. After the game, played in all weather, he and his wife, Et, entertained what came to be a generation of clerks, spouses, children and family members. The pinnacle of his fitness program was the 65-mile bicycle ride on his 65th birthday in 1998. Justice Clifford, then in his 74th year, was the only other member of the Court able to make the 65 miles. Similarly, Justice Stein led a 60-mile ride on his 60th birthday, again with Justice Clifford among the group.

We cannot speak of Justice Stein without speaking of Martha's Vineyard, a place where he vacationed. He did some of his best work on the porch of his beach house. In later years, after Chief Justice Deborah T. Poritz and Justice James H. Coleman Jr. joined the Court, we occasionally gathered at Justice Stein's Vineyard home to prepare for the new term.

8
The Mayor or the Monsignor

T his is what they called me. The first is a reference to my tenure from 1968 to 1978 as mayor of the Borough of Red Bank and frequent mention of experiences that related to cases before the Court. The second is a reference to my reputation for excising from Supreme Court opinions unnecessary graphic details in sex cases. I did not do so out of religious conviction but out of good taste. This is what Justice Clifford wrote in the spring of 2000 in a Rutgers Law Journal article on the occasion of my retirement:

> The man's a throw-back. He lives by the values of our forefathers: loyalty, devotion to duty, personal integrity, consideration toward others, that sort of thing. When he tells you the time of day, you don't need to look at your watch.

> On the Court, Justice O'Hern dealt in cosmic concepts. He saw the big picture. Quick to recognize where an issue fit in the greater scheme of things, he found a way to accommodate the devilish details

of a case to the Right Answer. He is a philosopher in the true sense of the word. Who will fill his place as the Conscience of the Court? Quiet and self-contained, this kind, gentle, thoughtful man can work a room with the best of them. Small wonder that he was elected mayor of Red Bank four times (an office, I learned just recently, that carried with it no salary). He is perfectly at ease with people of all stripes, and they with him — the champagne and caviar crowd as well as the shot-and-a-beer guys.

Which reminds me. It was Dan O'Hern who invented the "Sal's Tavern" test, now part of the permanent lore of the Court: a judicial opinion that does not make sense to the gang down at Sal's Tavern is unacceptable. Do it over.

None of the thirteen members of the Court with whom I served, with the possible exception of Justice Mark A. Sullivan, whom Justice O'Hern succeeded, worked with greater efficiency. The dispatch with which he churned out his assigned opinions was a source of astonishment to us all and of embarrassment to me, a world-class procrastinator. I don't know how much time he spent on the petitions for certification, but his conference notes on the petitions were an indecipherable maze of handwritten scribbles, folded-down pages from the opinion below, and one-word clues, the whole mess held together, sort of, by an elastic band. He alone could make sense out of them, and make great good sense he did in his recitations at conference.

By those who served with him Justice O'Hern will be remembered for having introduced the "chart" into the conference room. At the beginning of the Court's semi-weekly conference he would construct a chart, placed on an easel, containing columns for "pluses" and "minuses." He would generally list, before the conference started, various gaffes (real and imagined) committed by the members and others since last we had met — anything from a dopey memo generated by a member to a dizzy editorial product by our friends in the press. A frequent subject, generally aimed at Chief Justice Wilentz (who could not possibly have cared less), was the performance of the New York Jets, owned by the Chief's brother-in-law. Additions to the chart were made during the conference by one and all. They amounted to a running commentary covering the territory between the irreverent and the scandalous. I hope somebody saved the evidence for posterity.

Unlike W.C. Fields, Dan O'Hern likes dogs and little children. He is a sun worshipper. The move out of the family home in Red Bank after thirty years almost did him in, but his devoted family appears to have nursed him through that traumatic event. He still plays tennis regularly, bringing to the game enthusiasm, perseverance, and demonstrably indifferent talent.

He has no enemies.

He has so much of which to be so proud.

He believes deeply in the jury system, the Constitution, and the rule of law.

Those who have been privileged to know and work with him will always recall Dan O'Hern's warmth, dedication to the highest principles, and towering rectitude.

What else did I contribute to the Court during my tenure from 1981 to 2000? I leave that to others. I loved to unravel complex cases and to try to state their resolution in simple terms that would cover the essential elements of the disposition.

We all sought respect for our opinions. One of the long-running jokes on the Court was that "I got no respect" for mine. One frequent butt of such jokes was my opinion in *Ostrowski v. Azzara*. Ms. Ostrowski, a diabetic whose extremities were at risk, could not bend over to cut her toenails. So she went to a podiatrist, but part of her toe became infected after the procedure and she became very ill. A jury threw out her malpractice claim on grounds of contributory fault. I was accused of being a bleeding heart for pointing out that she may not have had the best of health habits, but none of us has a legal duty to adhere to a healthy diet or refrain from smoking. I was thrilled when *Corbin on Contracts* contained this squib about the case in its 2005 Spring Cumulative Supplement, Volume 11, Interim Edition, §1039 (Damages Are Not Recoverable for Avoidable Consequences) (A)(10):

Ostrowski v. Azzara, 111 N.J. 429, 545 A.2d 148 (1988). A diabetic, cigarette-smoking patient brought this medical malpractice action against the physician who had removed the toenail from her left big toe and, allegedly, caused the ultimate removal of her leg above the knee after bypass surgery had failed to correct the non-healing, pre-gangrenous wound left by the toenail surgery. The jury apportioned the fault at 51% that of the patient, thus disallowing any recovery. This finding was affirmed on appeal, but reversed and remanded for a new trial by the Supreme Court on review.

PHOTO BY BILL KOSTROUN

Daniel O'Hern liked to unravel complicated cases and state them in understandable terms because, he said, "The Court's survival as an institution depends on public acceptance of its opinions." He is shown here in 1995.

The court held that the doctrine of mitigation should not be permitted to disallow all recovery in such cases, saying that the jury was, thus, improperly instructed (a further problem was identified in that no distinction was made between pre-and post-operative conduct on the part of the patient, the court apparently indicating that pre-operative conduct would go to the issue of negligence, and post-operative conduct would go to the issue of mitigation). This analytical framework deserves study and the court is to be congratulated on its clear-headed handling of very complex legal issues. No blurring of negligence analysis and mitigation doctrine should be allowed, and this case shows how proper analysis can lead to the correct conclusion. I loved the clear-headed part.

PHOTO COURTESY OF DANIEL J. O'HERN

Daniel O'Hern, right, clerked for U.S. Supreme Court Justice William Brennan Jr. and admired his courage to take unpopular stands. They are shown in 1996 at a celebration of Brennan's 90th birthday.

I brought to the Court exposure to an array of human and commercial problems during my 20 years of private practice. I was born on May 23, 1930, in Red Bank and was raised there. At the time, Red Bank was a river town, one generation removed from the mythical River City immortalized in Meredith Wilson's play, *The Music Man*. Red Bank had all the flaws of Sinclair Lewis' *Main Street*. Until the 1930s, its schools were segregated, and until the 1940s, the movie house was as well. World War II changed everything. The Sigmund Eisner Company, a military uniform factory, and the Fort Monmouth Signal School were the dominant employers in Red Bank. I graduated from Fordham College in 1951 and Harvard Law School in 1957. My practice in Red Bank ran the spectrum from matters involving corporations, beverage distributors and regional food chains to family and criminal cases.

My political career paralleled the 1960s civil rights movement. We experienced civil unrest in Red Bank not unlike the riots of Newark and Plainfield in 1967. Involvement in politics led me to know all the black ministers in Red Bank and to recognize the contributions of their churches to the fabric of our society. Appreciation for their values had a profound effect on my perceptions of equality.

Aside from family, there were two important figures in my life. The first was U.S. Supreme Court Justice William J. Brennan Jr. At the time I was attending Harvard Law School, Justice Brennan was a member of the New Jersey Supreme Court. In 1956, he had moved his chambers to Red Bank, and I had hoped to be able to serve a judicial clerkship with him. In October 1956, I met Paul A. Freund, one of my law school professors, on the street in Cambridge. He said, "You must be very proud that your

New Jersey justice was appointed to the United States Supreme Court." I responded, "I'm a little disappointed because I wanted to be one of his clerks in New Jersey." Professor Freund looked at me and asked, "Are you still interested?" I said it would be a stretch for me, as I was not on the Harvard Law Review. Professor Freund replied, "Well, I pick his clerks," and that is the story of how I came to clerk for Justice Brennan.

From Justice Brennan, I learned that respect for the law requires courage. He suffered rejection by his peers for his unflinching insistence that the judiciary was to stand between the citizen and the state and to ensure that constitutional guarantees were enforced, no matter how unpopular the judge's views. Only one who loved his country deeply could hold that it was unconstitutional to make it a crime to burn the American flag. In the 1989 flag-burning case, *Texas v. Johnson*, Justice Brennan wrote "[that] ... the speaker's opinion ... gives offense ... is a reason for according it constitutional protection" because "free speech under our system of government ... best serves its high purpose when it induces a condition of unrest, creates dissatisfaction with conditions as they are, or even stirs people to anger."

The Court's decision, he said, "reaffirms the principles of freedom and inclusiveness that the flag best reflects, ... and ... the conviction that our tolera[nce] ... is a sign and source of our strength. Indeed, one of the proudest images of our flag, the one immortalized in our own national anthem[ ] is of the bombardment it survived at Fort McHenry. It is the Nation's resilience, not its rigidity, that Texas sees reflected in the flag — and it is that resilience that we reassert today."

He also had a playful side, as seen in 1984 when his son, New Jersey State Bar Association President William J. Brennan III, persuaded him to speak before the organization's midyear meeting in London. While there, my wife, Barbara, offered to introduce Justice Brennan to Jim Zazzali. Understandably, Zazzali was delighted because the Justice had been a friend of his father, Andrew Zazzali, head of the Office of Price Stabilization in the Truman administration. In addition, Jim had appeared before the U.S. Supreme Court the year before in *NLRB v. Bildisco & Bildisco*, in which he argued that collective bargaining agreements should survive in bankruptcy. On being introduced, Justice Brennan said, "Of course I remember your dad," and he related several complimentary memories.

Zazzali responded that he had greatly enjoyed arguing in *Bildisco*, even though he had lost the key issue in a 5-4 vote, with Justice Brennan writing the dissent. And then, with his impish Irish countenance and gracious smile, Justice Brennan took Zazzali's head between his hands and vigorously patted him on the cheeks. "Jimmy, we almost beat 'em. We almost beat 'em."

We took our children to visit Justice Brennan in his chambers from time to time and although many years could go by without a trip, Justice Brennan always maintained a keen interest in our family. Two incidents, in particular, show the genuine warmth he extended.

In 1984, Justice Brennan was invited to speak at Harvard Law School, where our daughter Eileen was in her first year. He had finished speaking and was proceeding down a hallway when Eileen called out, "Justice Brennan,

Justice Brennan. Hi, it's Eileen O'Hern." He stopped, took Eileen under his arm and walked with her all the way down the hallway. In 1988, I took our son Jim, then in his second year at Seton Hall University School of Law, to observe arguments before the U.S. Supreme Court. I had arranged for us to see Justice Brennan beforehand. Jim reached the reception area before I did and was nervous that this legal giant would not remember him. But the Justice came out and said, "Jimmy! How are you?" He gave one of his warm handshakes and asked, "Where's the old man?" When Jim said he was not sure, the Justice responded, "Forget about him. He'll find his way." He acted as though they were old friends.

Those encounters were examples of the affection Justice Brennan had for our family and for the families of other clerks. I cannot recall an occasion or reunion when he did not greet a clerk's spouse by his or her first name.

He was filled with so much life and joy. He made you feel good to be in his presence.

The second person who influenced my life was Brendan Byrne, governor of New Jersey from 1973 to 1981. From Gov. Byrne I learned the importance of leadership. A somewhat trivial story illustrates the point. I once was with him at the Monmouth Park Racetrack when a number of people came up to ask for his betting advice. After a while I said to him, "Governor, why do they come to you for advice on betting the horses?" He said, "Dan, the leader has to have a plan." I never forgot that. He was a leader with a plan in so many ways.

His preservation of the Pinelands was a prime example.

In the center of New Jersey, America's most densely populated state, there existed 1 million acres of forest farms
in a scenic area known as the Pinelands. In 1967, John
McPhee concluded in his book, *The Pine Barrens*, that
little could be done to save the region. He wrote that the
Pinelands "seemed to be headed slowly for extinction."
After Gov. Byrne took office, he asked McPhee, "Do you
really think it's hopeless?" When McPhee answered "yes,"
Gov. Byrne said, "I'll see about that," and he did.

A unique partnership eventually saved the Pinelands.
In 1978, Congress created the Pinelands National Reserve,
a place where governments at every level from national
agencies to local planning boards could help shape the region's future, in keeping with some basic guidelines. On
Feb. 8, 1979, Gov. Byrne issued an executive order creat-
ing the Pinelands Commission, and in June of that year,
at his request, the Legislature supplemented the federal
law by passing the Pinelands Protection Act.

Gov. Byrne had courage. At one point as commissioner
of the Department of Environmental Protection in his
administration, I went to inspect conditions at Liberty
State Park in Jersey City and returned shocked. I told the
Governor it would cost a lot of money to repair the shat-
tered terminals, rotting piers and other structures. He
said to me, "Dan, don't worry about the money. Just do it."

He was a delight to work for, from the moment of my
initial interview with him for the DEP job — both of us
bundled up in the sunlight in February 1978 next to the
pool at the governor's mansion. He selected me as his chief
counsel in 1979 and named me to the Court in 1981, where
I remained until 2000.

PHOTO BY OFFICE OF PUBLIC COMMUNICATIONS, STATE OF NEW JERSEY

Daniel O'Hern considered Brendan Byrne a major influence in his life because of the governor's leadership abilities. Byrne, seated third from the left, is shown signing the Pinelands Protection Act in June 1979. O'Hern, standing fourth from the right, was the commissioner of the state Department of Environmental Protection at the time.

Gov. Byrne was possessed of a preternatural calm. When I asked Dottie Seltzer, his personal secretary, about this, she said, "Dan, he dodged a bullet when he was serving as a navigator in World War II." She told of a mission over Germany when his plane was hit. He had leaned forward for a moment and then back. As he did, a shell came into the cockpit at the spot he had just vacated. She said he told her, "I just resolved not to worry about things. There is nothing that you can do about it." In comparison, other matters seemed inconsequential. He was fearless.

When I asked him about his calm nature, he said, "The Pope has bigger problems than I do."

Gov. Byrne also had a disarming style of being gubernatorial. If he wanted to signal to me that a meeting should end, he would grab a baseball bat or shine his shoes.

I would never have succeeded as his chief counsel if we did not have the same life rhythms. We were morning people. He left the Statehouse each day at about 4 p.m., and, with a gaggle of reporters surrounding him, would say to us, "hang in there." It is advice I have since given to others.

PHOTO COURTESY OF DANIEL J. O'HERN

Daniel O'Hern figured out how to accommodate the "devilish details of a case to the Right Answer," Robert Clifford wrote in the Rutgers Law Journal. O'Hern is shown at right with his wife, Barbara, while taking his tenure oath in 1988 before Robert Wilentz.

9
The Clark

N o court can be supreme without the help of many others, and we had the best. The head of our administrative staff was Stephen W. Townsend, the clerk of the New Jersey Supreme Court. We called him the Clark; it was Justice Clifford's way of making us sound like a British court. I often told Townsend he was wasting his time with us, that he could have made $250,000 a year with a Wall Street law firm. He is witty and brilliant, but most of all wise.

The clerk never sits with the justices when they deliberate on opinion assignments or on circulating opinions, but our discussions on opinions usually overlap with other discussions on motions, certifications and calendar matters. Townsend never interjected himself into our discussions, but an arched eyebrow, a furrowed brow or a change in the tone of his voice told us all we needed to know.

The custom of the Court was for the Clerk's Office to prepare memoranda summarizing the thousands of motions and hundreds of cases of attorney-discipline we reviewed each year. Townsend's memos were gems, laced with humor, sometimes sarcasm, but always correct and to the point. Here is one:

SUPREME COURT OF NEW JERSEY

OFFICE OF THE CLERK

DATE: January 20, 1998

INTEROFFICE MEMORANDUM
TO: Supreme Court
FROM: Stephen W. Townsend
RE: M-650-97 William Fleuhr v. City of Cape May
(A-136-97)
Nature of Motion: M-650 Appear amicus curiae
Moving Party: Surfrider Foundation and Surfers'
Environmental Alliance-SEA

History: The Court granted cert in this case in
October. It will be argued later in the term (probably March). The issues involve municipal immu-
nity for liability for injuries to swimmers in heavy
surf. "Negligent supervision" features prominently
in the argument of counsel.

The within motion was filed 1/14/98. In it, movants explain that they are world-wide non-profit
organizations that are "devoted to the protection
and enhancement of the world's ocean resources
through research, education and activism." The
New Jersey chapter has been involved in many
beach access issues, particularly as they relate to
surfing.

Movants wish to file a brief and participate in oral argument on the appeal. Movants are opposed to the "closing" of the ocean to surfers during "high surf" conditions. They have prepared legislation that was prefiled for the 1998 session of the Senate.

RECOMMENDATION: Throw your boogie boards in your woodies and have movants join the fun.

And here is another:

SUPREME COURT OF NEW JERSEY OFFICE OF THE CLERK

DATE: February 22, 1995

INTEROFFICE MEMORANDUM

TO: Supreme Court

FROM: Stephen W. Townsend RE: M-***

Nature of Motion: Leave to file a brief and argue amicus curiae

• • •

Counsel for movants filed the attached. In it,

movants argue that their participation in the appeal will assist the Court. They contend that they are dedicated to protecting freedom of information rights and the First Amendment interests of the news media. Their participation, including oral argument, is sought as a means of ensuring that the Court has the benefit of their valuable insights and arguments.

RECOMMENDATION: Grant the motion, limited to the filing of a brief. If you let one [party] in, you may get a ton of applications you do not really want. That having been said, however, if [Attorney A or B requests it], I would let either or both of them argue. If that demonstrates some sort of bias, why then who among us is free from the taint that encumbers the human condition? As Shakespeare once said to Christopher Marlowe at the opening night of Much Ado About Nothing, "Let she who is without sin stone the first cast." Grant "brief only" and then — Exeunt all, stage left.

Townsend knew the foibles of the justices, especially the claim by several of them to be tennis players. In this expurgated disciplinary matter, he feigned to appeal to these justices' latent favoritism for tennis players:

With no more than an arched eyebrow or a change in the tone of his voice, Court Clerk Stephen Townsend let his sentiments be known in cases before the Court. He is shown here in the late 1980s or early 1990s.

SUPREME COURT OF NEW JERSEY
OFFICE OF THE CLERK
DATE: March 10, 1986
INTEROFFICE MEMORANDUM
TO: Supreme Court
FROM: Stephen W. Townsend
RE: D-IMO

• • •

The DRB [Disciplinary Review Board] recommends a three-month suspension for respondent based on his conviction for presenting a fraudulent document to a court. Mitigating factors kept the suspension at a minimum.

• • •

Respondent was admitted to the bar in ****. He had no prior disciplinary history.

In the ethics proceedings, respondent essentially admitted all charges against him.

• • •

Respondent sought to mitigate the sanction against him by listing a host of personal problems. The record was not entirely clear about the timing of some of these problems, but the DRB was persuaded that several of them affected respondent's actions. Among the problems raised were:

1. Severe depression, including an involuntary commitment between July and August;

2. A replacement of his right hip;

3. A later replacement of his left hip;

4. His wife's desertion and subsequent action for divorce (no date given);

5. His resistance to taking the medication prescribed for his bi-polar condition; and

6. His inability to play tennis any longer, which seriously affected his self-image. He had played tournament-level tennis since **** and "had become a well-known and respected player."

The DRB noted that there were indications of alcohol abuse and gambling excess in the record but that respondent had not relied on those problems as mitigating factors.

The DRB concluded that respondent's "serious" misconduct merited a suspension. Only numerous "compelling" mitigating factors led the Board to recommend a three-month suspension.

RECOMMENDATION: Thank God for tennis! If this guy played recreation b-ball or senior hockey, he would have been down the tube. I note that many of his "mitigating factors" actually involve events or additional stress that occurred after the criminal acts that are the basis of the ethics charges against him. As Gussie Moran once said to Bobby Riggs, "What a racquet!"

I have several recommendations.

1. Tennis-playing Justices should not recuse themselves on the basis that they can relate to respondent's loss of self-image (we would lose a quorum).

2. The report and recommendation of the DRB should be accepted and respondent suspended for three months.

3. The Order of suspension should provide that respondent must demonstrate that he is physically
   and mentally fit to return to the practice of law before he can be reinstated. A proctorship should be
   imposed, if deemed necessary by the DRB at that
   time.

Here was Townsend's response to a question of whether
Justice Stein and I could fit a trip to the French Open into
the Court's schedule:

SUPREME COURT OF NEW JERSEY
OFFICE OF THE CLERK
DATE: March 10, 1999

INTEROFFICE MEMORANDUM
TO: Justice O'Hern
Justice Stein
FROM: Stephen W. Townsend
RE: 1999 French Open

Mirabilé dictu! Q'est ce que c'est? Il est une ideé
formidable. Les Open Français est 24 Mai au 6
Juin, 1999. Pas mal. Nous avons ici une conference
sur 25 Mai; quel dommage. Ah, peutêtre une petite
adjustement? Pah. Non, non, non. Avez-vous sat-
isfé? Bon.[2]

[1]Okay. The Open runs from May 24 to June 6. We
have a conference on May 25. Well, what the heck;
who needs to see the first couple of days, anyhow.

You could go after Memorial Day (May 31) and catch the last five or six days; i.e., the best stuff.

[2]The foregoing information is compliments of Phyllis Townsend, by way of those wonderful folks at the Ewing Branch of the Mercer County Library. The pigdin French is all mine. Merde.

Townsend's relationship with Chief Justice Wilentz is hard to put into words. There was a mock formality to it when we were together at conferences exchanging thoughts about Court business. The Chief Justice would sometimes show displeasure when Townsend offered a contrary suggestion. It was an occasion for us to ask in feigned exasperation: "Who do you think is running this Court, Chief? — You or Stephen?"

But the clerk and his entire staff were invaluable contributors to the greatness of the Wilentz Court. Our elbow clerks (the young men and women who worked with us for one year after law school) worked under Townsend's supervision. Their contributions to the work of the Court were immense. They were bright, idealistic and committed aides. I hesitate to name any without naming all, but I will mention a few. Jack Sabatino, one of Justice Garibaldi's clerks, is now an Appellate Division judge. Peter Verniero was a clerk for Justice Clifford, served as state attorney general before he became a member of our Court and now is in private practice. John Farmer Jr. was a death-penalty clerk for two terms, served as state attorney general and senior counsel to the 9/11 Commission, and now is the dean at Rutgers Law School-Newark. Janine Bauer was our first death-penalty clerk and now is in private practice.

New clerks were a joy to us each term, bringing fresh insights and dogged preparation for the most part. And they enjoyed working for the Court.

10

The Past as Predictor

At either end of the 15 years I have described, I served with exceptional justices. If the current Court were permitted to serve an uninterrupted span of years, equivalent to those of the Weintraub and Wilentz courts, I am sure it would achieve the same national distinction.

Justice Morris Pashman was an outstanding jurist. In the 13 months I served with him, he wrote many significant opinions. *Hill v. Hill* held that when a wife earned the money to support the marital household while the husband obtained his professional degree and license, a fair measure of rehabilitation should be given to her. In *General Assembly v. Byrne*, Justice Pashman strengthened the separation of powers by invalidating the Legislative Oversight Act because it impeded the executive in its constitutional mandate to execute the laws faithfully. In *Maressa v. New Jersey Monthly*, he wrote to sustain the freedom of the press.

Justice Sidney M. Schreiber, with whom I served for three years, was a workhorse of the Court, with perhaps the broadest practice experience of any member. *In re*

Conroy carefully crafted the standards for determining the right to die. *Dickinson v. Fund for the Support of Public Schools* invalidated a constitutional amendment that was a giveaway of state lands. And *Matthews v. Bay Head Improvement Association* sustained the interest of citizens to beach access. These were major national decisions.

In the four years I served with Chief Justice Poritz, she demonstrated a similar capacity to write nationally important precedent. In *Dale v. Boy Scouts of America*, she wrote that the Boy Scouts did not have the constitutional right to exclude the plaintiff from participation in the organization as a scoutmaster solely because of his sexual preference. Although the U.S. Supreme Court later reversed, it appears to have been a hollow victory for the Boy Scouts in that the many groups that had previously supported the organization were dismayed by its expressly discriminatory policy. In *New Jersey Transit PBA Local 304 v. New Jersey Transit Corporation*, Chief Justice Poritz established national standards for drug testing in safety-sensitive positions.

During the six years I served with Justice James H. Coleman Jr., he showed the ability to write significant opinions. In *Brill v. Guardian Life Insurance Company of America*, he renewed the standards for grant of summary judgment. In *State v. Carty*, he drove the nail into racial profiling by holding that traffic stops must be based on a reasonably articulable suspicion. While on the Appellate Division, he foreshadowed the U.S. Supreme Court decision in *Batson v. Kentucky*, holding in *State v. Gilmore* that the race-based exercise of pre-emptory challenges in criminal trials violated the constitutional rights of defendants.

I had less than one full term to serve with Justices Verniero, Virginia Long and Jaynee LaVecchia, Gov. Whitman's choices to succeed Justices Pollock, Handler and Garibaldi. And of course, I did not serve with James R. Zazzali, whom Gov. Whitman nominated to succeed me and whom Gov. Jon Corzine later nominated as Chief Justice. Each demonstrated or has demonstrated the capacity to continue the Court's traditions.

I will say that the Court's work becomes harder as the years go by because of the increase in volume. For example, the worksheet for the Court's first conference for the 1957-58 term had 16 motions, 15 petitions for certification and one case of attorney discipline. The first conference of the 1999-2000 term, on the other hand, had 20 motions, 92 petitions for certification and six cases of attorney discipline.

PHOTO BY NEW JERSEY SUPREME COURT

The members of the Court posed in the conference room with their clerks for the 1999-2000 term. Seated at center is Deborah Poritz, with Gary Stein on the left and Daniel O'Hern on the right. Standing from left, starting behind Stein, are Jaynee LaVecchia, Peter Verniero, Virginia Long and James Coleman Jr.

11

What Makes a Court Supreme

$\mathbf{F}$irst, I will candidly admit that judging judges is a bit like judging figure skaters; a lot is in the eye of the beholder. Harvard Law School Professor Paul Freund offered worthy advice in his review of *Cardozo: A Study in Reputation*, a book by Judge Richard Posner of the Seventh U.S. Circuit Court of Appeals. "Reputation and merit are not always the closest of companions. John Chipman Gray, a professor of law at Harvard at the turn of the century, conferred this encomium on his early predecessor Joseph Story: he was 'a man of great learning, and of reputation for learning greater even than the learning itself,'" Freund wrote in *The New York Times* on Nov. 4, 1990.

No member of the New Jersey Supreme Court was a demigod in the vein of Justices Benjamin Cardozo or Oliver Wendell Holmes Jr. Like the casts of the television shows "Cheers" or "Seinfeld," to which my clerks introduced me, the ensemble possessed qualities that enabled it to succeed as a group.

The most important characteristic of a quality court is the courage to follow the law in spite of the greatest of pressures. In *In the Matter of Randolph*, quoting from S. Rep. No. 711, 75th Cong., 1st Sess. 14 (1937) (rejecting the Court-packing plan), the New Jersey Supreme Court summed up the ideal of judicial independence in 1986:

[W]e would rather have an independent Court, a fearless Court, a Court that will dare to announce its honest opinions in what it believes to be the defense of liberties of the people, than a Court that, out of fear or sense of obligation to the appointing power, or factional passion, approves any measure we may enact.

In his resignation letter to Gov. Whitman on June 13, 1996, Chief Justice Wilentz expressed concern for the judiciary. He wrote:

We have a fine court system, still supported by the people of New Jersey in these somewhat difficult times. That support is one of our most important sources of strength. The ultimate source of our strength and integrity remains our own commitment to judicial independence, total and uncompromising.

A second important quality in a court is a breadth of perception, the residue of human experience that enables a judge to place issues in perspective. A judge whose entire career has been limited to the defense of antitrust cases will perhaps not grasp the proper relationship among the branches of government. Our Court had members with broad experience in public and private life, attained through a diversified legal practice, teaching or a combination of public service and private practice. Judicial experience is a factor to be considered in supporting nominees to the Court, but should not be the determinative factor. For example, trial experience is often regarded as an important qualification for bench. Yet, Learned Hand, generally regarded as the greatest judge never to have sat on the U.S. Supreme Court, was an ineffective and somewhat inexperienced trial lawyer. The point is simply this: Experience is not the best predictor of performance.

In his book, Judge Posner attributes much of Justice Cardozo's reputation to his skill with words. Judge Posner said that when Justice Cardozo, as a member of the New York Court of Appeals, wrote in criticism of the exclusionary rule, "the criminal is to go free because the constable has blundered," he was able to "pack into a simple sentence of eleven words the entire case against the exclusionary rule."

Next in order of importance is a natural intelligence. On our Court there are occasions when profoundly difficult, technical issues must be resolved. For example, at the end of my service, we had to master the intricacies of DNA evidence. Justices Handler and Pollock devoted months to unraveling the scientific issues. You have to be smart to understand some things.

The next trait on my list is collegiality. The hallmark of the New Jersey Supreme Court — at least for the 15 years in which I knew it — was its willingness to talk its cases through. We called it "wrestling the case to the ground." It was our custom to debate cases for hours, and sometimes days, until we exhausted every aspect of the analysis. Judges must be willing to participate in that type of discussion for a court to be great. This requires qualities of open-mindedness, a willingness to hear both sides of an argument. The quality of a judge's interaction with colleagues and his or her patience and evenhanded-ness will greatly contribute to the work of the court. It is one thing to be firm; it is another to simply be stubborn and heavy-handed.

PHOTO BY STEPHEN W. TOWNSEND

Farewell dinners, this one for Gary Stein and James Coleman Jr. in May 2003, included spouses. Standing, from left, are Ruth Clifford, Barbara O'Hern, Lisa Verniero, Rose Marie Handler, Eileen Zazzali, Phyllis Townsend, Alan Poritz, Jonathan Weiner (Virginia Long's husband), Michael Cole (Jaynee LaVecchia's husband), and Sophia Coleman. Seated, from left, are Et Stein, Ruth Schreiber and Barbara Wallace.

A judge must be able to express legal principles in clear and forceful language, an attribute described by Gerald Gunther in his biography, *Learned Hand: The Man and the Judge*. The author portrayed Judge Hand as "the consummate judicial craftsman, if judicial craftsmanship is understood as the ability to construct eloquent, persuasive legal arguments, to draw meaningful and imaginative analogies from related fields of law or human endeavor, to clarify muddled legal doctrines, to give scrupulous attention to the facts, and to master the technical aspects of a case," Michael J. Gerhardt wrote in a review of the book in 80 Cornell L. Rev. 1627 (1995).

A little bit of self-doubt is also useful. Justice Holmes said, in a speech on Feb. 15, 1913, before the Harvard Law School Association of New York:

> We too need education in the obvious — to learn to transcend our own convictions and to leave room for much that we hold dear to be done away with short of revolution by the orderly change of law.

Finally, in my view, a good sense of humor is a sign of a great mind. Not only is humor an indicator of intelligence, it can play an important part in the work of a collegial court. One example was our conference discussion of *Opinion 688*, a difficult case of attorney-client privilege. Justice Clifford started the discussion. Next in order was Justice Handler. He began, "I agree with everything Bob has said except his conclusion and his reasoning."

The Court's survival as an institution depends on public acceptance of its opinions. We have no soldiers or police who can arrest a governor or force a legislator to vote for additional funds for schools. Justice Handler explained our authority this way, in "A Matter of Opinion," 15 Rutgers L.J. 1 (1983):

> In understanding the role and purpose of the judicial opinion, a central theme that we must appreciate is that the judicial power is a vital and sensitive one. Moreover, that power is not truly a popular one. The importance of the judiciary is derived from its constitutional status as an equal branch of government and its function as a supporting and separating arch between the other branches of government. The judiciary must constantly and affirmatively establish in the regular exercise of its power its own legitimacy. That legitimacy must be revealed by the rightness and acceptability of its actions. It must be self-evident.

A public that seeks a court that is truly supreme must search for judges who can make self-evident the legitimacy of the court's actions. To that end, a governor or judicial selection committee should seek men and women with demonstrated qualities of independence of mind, the courage to sustain that independence, the breadth of experience to have witnessed most of the issues that affect the lives of our citizens, natural intelligence to understand these issues and the acquired skill of being able to explain the reasons for judgment. The Chief Justice must be the nonpareil among members, often recalled in the mold of Arthur T. Vanderbilt or Joseph Weintraub. The Court must respect its leader. He or she must keep the Court on its course. For the Wilentz Court, the distant star toward which we all aimed was public confidence in the judiciary and the legal profession.

When a warm sense of humor and genuine collegiality is added to the mix, a fine court is the result. We shared many family occasions as a court — weddings, birthdays, dinner parties and even gala visits to the New York Athletic Club as guests of Justice Garibaldi, who had helped open it to women. Another memorable occasion was "The Hookers Party." Justice Handler's wife, Rose Marie, had invited the justices' spouses to the family farm to learn how to weave hooked rugs, and after our Court session, we joined the gathering for dinner.

I once said to Justice Pollock, "maybe we are too close to each other to be a good court." He replied, "Dan, contented cows give the best milk."

I am convinced that among the diverse people of New Jersey, there are many lawyers and judges who possess these qualities in abundance. A well-stocked judiciary will provide a pool of this talent. I have met so many exemplary lawyers who are discouraged from seeking judicial office by the current selection process. A strong governor has many trump cards to play and need not yield to senatorial courtesy or political considerations. He or she need only seek out the many fine candidates.

www.ingramcontent.com/pod-product-compliance
Lightning Source LLC
Chambersburg PA
CBHW030631220526
45463CB00004B/1486

www.ingramcontent.com/pod-product-compliance
Lightning Source LLC
Chambersburg PA
CBHW072048230526
45468CB00019B/1048